# INSTITUTE OF PACIFIC RELATIONS

## INQUIRY SERIES

# THE INSTITUTE OF PACIFIC RELATIONS

*The Institute of Pacific Relations is an unofficial and non-political body, founded in 1925 to facilitate the scientific study of the peoples of the Pacific Area. It is composed of National Councils in eleven countries.*

*The Institute as such and the National Councils of which it is composed are precluded from expressing an opinion on any aspect of national or international affairs; opinions expressed in this study are, therefore, purely individual.*

## NATIONAL COUNCILS OF THE INSTITUTE

*American Council, Institute of Pacific Relations*

*Australian Institute of International Affairs*

*Canadian Institute of International Affairs*

*China Institute of Pacific Relations*

*Comité d'Études des Problèmes du Pacifique*

*Japanese Council, Institute of Pacific Relations*

*Netherlands-Netherlands Indies Council, Institute of Pacific Relations*

*New Zealand Institute of International Affairs*

*Philippine Council, Institute of Pacific Relations*

*Royal Institute of International Affairs*

*U.S.S.R. Council, Institute of Pacific Relations*

# THE PROBLEM OF JAPANESE TRADE EXPANSION IN THE POST-WAR SITUATION

*Some Other Studies Already Completed in the*
*I. P. R. Inquiry Series*

# THE PROBLEM OF JAPANESE TRADE EXPANSION IN THE POST-WAR SITUATION

*By*

## MIRIAM S. FARLEY

*I. P. R. INQUIRY SERIES*

INTERNATIONAL SECRETARIAT

INSTITUTE OF PACIFIC RELATIONS

PUBLICATIONS OFFICE, 129 EAST 52ND STREET, NEW YORK

1940

# FOREWORD

This study forms part of the documentation of an Inquiry organized by the Institute of Pacific Relations into the problems arising from the conflict in the Far East.

It has been prepared by Miss Miriam S. Farley of the research staff of the American Council, Institute of Pacific Relations.

The study has been submitted in draft to a number of authorities including the following, many of whom made suggestions and criticisms which were of great value in the process of revision: Professor Eugene Staley, Mr. T. A. Bisson, and Dr. Charles B. Fahs.

Though many of the comments received have been incorporated in the final text, the above authorities do not of course accept responsibility for the study. The statements of fact or of opinion appearing herein do not represent the views of the Institute of Pacific Relations or of the Pacific Council or of any of the National Councils. Such statements are made on the sole responsibility of the author. The Japanese Council has not found it possible to participate in the Inquiry, and assumes, therefore, no responsibility either for its results or for its organization.

During 1938 the Inquiry was carried on under the general direction of Dr. J. W. Dafoe as Chairman of the Pacific Council and in 1939 under his successor, Dr. Philip C. Jessup. Every member of the International Secretariat has contributed to the research and editorial work in connection with the Inquiry, but special mention should be made of Mr. W. L. Holland, Miss Kate Mitchell and Miss Hilda Austern, who have carried the major share of this responsibility.

In the general conduct of this Inquiry into the problems arising from the conflict in the Far East the Institute has benefited by the counsel of the following Advisers:

Professor H. F. Angus of the University of British Columbia

Dr. J. B. Condliffe of the London School of Economics

M. Etienne Dennery of the Ecole des Sciences Politiques.

These Advisers have co-operated with the Chairman and the Secretary-General in an effort to insure that the publications issued in connection with the Inquiry conform to a proper standard of sound and impartial scholarship. Each manuscript has been submitted to at least two of the Advisers and although they do not necessarily subscribe to the statements or views in this or any of the studies, they consider this study to be a useful contribution to the subject of the Inquiry.

The purpose of this Inquiry is to relate unofficial scholarship to the problems arising from the present situation in the Far East. Its purpose is to provide members of the Institute in all countries and the members of I.P.R. Conferences with an impartial and constructive analysis of the situation in the Far East with a view to indicating the major issues which must be considered in any future adjustment of international relations in that area. To this end, the analysis will include an account of the economic and political conditions which produced the situation existing in July 1937, with respect to China, to Japan and to the other foreign Powers concerned; an evaluation of developments during the war period which appear to indicate important trends in the policies and programs of all the Powers in relation to the Far Eastern situation; and, finally, an estimate of the principal political, economic and social conditions which may be expected in a post-war period, the possible forms of adjustment which might be applied under these conditions, and the effects of such adjustments upon the countries concerned.

The Inquiry does not propose to "document" a specific plan for dealing with the Far Eastern situation. Its aim is to focus available information on the present crisis in forms which will be useful to those who lack either the time or the expert knowledge to study the vast amount of material now appearing or already published in a number of languages. Attention may also be drawn to a series of studies on topics bearing on the Far Eastern situation which is being prepared by the Japanese Council. That series is being undertaken entirely independently of this Inquiry, and for its organization and publication the Japanese Council alone is responsible.

The present study, "The Problem of Japanese Trade Expansion in the Post-War Situation," falls within the framework of the second of the four general groups of studies which it is proposed to make as follows:

I. The political and economic conditions which have contributed to the present course of the policies of Western Powers in the Far East; their territorial and economic interests; the effects on their Far Eastern policies of internal economic and political developments and of developments in their foreign policies vis-a-vis other parts of the world; the probable effects of the present conflict on their positions in the Far East; their changing attitudes and policies with respect to their future relations in that area.

II. The political and economic conditions which have contributed to the present course of Japanese foreign policy and possible important future developments; the extent to which Japan's policy toward China has been influenced by Japan's geographic conditions and material resources, by special features in the political and economic organization of Japan which directly or indirectly affect the formulation of her present foreign policy, by economic and political developments in China, by the external policies of other Powers affecting Japan; the principal political, economic and social factors which may be expected in a post-war Japan; possible and probable adjustments on the part of other nations which could aid in the solution of Japan's fundamental problems.

III. The political and economic conditions which have contributed to the present course of Chinese foreign policy and possible important future developments; Chinese unification and reconstruction, 1931-37, and steps leading toward the policy of united national resistance to Japan; the present degree of political cohesion and economic strength; effects of resistance and current developments on the position of foreign interests in China and changes in China's relations with foreign Powers; the principal political, economic and social factors which may be expected in a post-war China;

possible and probable adjustments on the part of other nations which could aid in the solution of China's fundamental problems.

IV. Possible methods for the adjustment of specific problems, in the light of information and suggestions presented in the three studies outlined above; analysis of previous attempts at bilateral or multilateral adjustments of political and economic relations in the Pacific and causes of their success or failure; types of administrative procedures and controls already tried out and their relative effectiveness; the major issues likely to require international adjustment in a post-war period and the most hopeful methods which might be devised to meet them; necessary adjustments by the Powers concerned; the basic requirements of a practical system of international organization which could promote the security and peaceful development of the countries of the Pacific area.

Edward C. Carter
*Secretary-General*

*New York,*
*January 17, 1940*

# CONTENTS

*Page*

# THE PROBLEM OF JAPANESE TRADE EXPANSION IN THE POST-WAR SITUATION

# INTRODUCTION

During the years immediately preceding the outbreak of the Sino-Japanese war the question of Japanese trade expansion emerged as an increasingly prominent and disturbing factor in international relations. Indeed, friction engendered by the grievances, real or imaginary, to which this question gave rise must be reckoned not least among the causes which have brought about the present crisis in the Pacific area. At present obscured by more urgent issues arising out of the hostilities in China, it remains one of the basic unsolved problems of the Far East.

Though extraordinarily complex in detail, the issues involved in the problem of Japanese trade expansion are clear enough in broad outline. Leaving out of consideration exaggerated claims and those of special interests, the essential issue may be simply stated. On the one hand there is Japan's claim that, owing to the peculiarities of her geographic, demographic and economic position, continuous expansion of her foreign trade is absolutely necessary for the maintenance of a tolerable standard of living among her people, to say nothing of improving that standard. On the other hand is the claim of Japan's neighbors that growing exports of cheap Japanese goods constitute a serious threat to established industries, desirable infant industries and existing standards of living in other countries. Is this conflict of economic nationalisms essentially irreconcilable?

Viewed in a broader perspective, the problem of adjustment raised by the economic evolution of Japan is merely part of the larger problem presented by industrially young countries whose productive powers are increasing faster than those of older industrial nations. This process is going on all over the world, and is paralleled by the rise of new industries or new producing areas within national boundaries. The international problems which it creates are not dissimilar to those presented, for example, by the shift of United States textile production from the northern to the southern states, or the rise of motor transport as a serious competitor to the American railroads. Constant readjustments, constant reallocation of capital, labor and natural

3

resources, constant shifts in the nature and direction of exchange of goods and services both within and across national boundaries, are necessary if economic organization is to keep pace with new discoveries and wider application of industrial technology.

In Japan's case, however, the economic issues are sharpened and complicated by the fact that both Japan and her competitors are sovereign states, amenable, in the existing state of international organization, to little or no social control. There are few means available at present by which international society can either determine or enforce upon its members such economic readjustments as would be dictated by a long-range view of their own best interests as well as those of the international society as a whole. Furthermore, a sovereign state, especially one possessing the strength and traditional psychology of a great power, has the opportunity of expressing dissatisfaction with its economic situation by means which, if perhaps no more constructive, are considerably more disturbing to international harmony than those which are open to private or sectional interests within a national state. The problem of regulating international trade in accordance with the requirements of a dynamic economic system is thus at once more difficult, and more urgent, than the same problem arising in the purely domestic sphere. It is, moreover, merely one of a complex of economic and political problems, all of which are intimately interrelated, which will demand attention in connection with any post-war settlement in the Far East.

In the present memorandum an attempt is made to focus attention on the problem of Japanese trade expansion in the post-war period. It has not been thought necessary to recount in detail the historical evolution of Japanese foreign trade. A summary picture is given in the appended tables, and numerous descriptive and analytical accounts are available covering developments prior to the present war.[1] It has seemed desirable, however, to describe in somewhat greater detail the repercussions of the war upon Japan's foreign trade, and to indicate briefly the nature of already apparent changes in her economic

[1] See for example T. Uyeda, *The Recent Development of Japanese Foreign Trade* (Japanese Council, I.P.R., Tokyo, 1936); G. E. Hubbard, *Eastern Industrialization and Its Effect on the West* (revised ed., Royal Institute of International Affairs, London, 1938); Mitsubishi Economic Research Bureau, *Japanese Trade and Industry* (London, 1936).

structure, induced by the war, which are likely to affect the future development of her commercial relations with other countries. Such an account will be found in Part I below, which incidentally may throw some light on Japan's present economic position. Part II represents an effort, necessarily tentative at the present time, to state the problem of Japanese trade expansion in the terms in which it is likely to present itself after the close of hostilities, and to review various methods which have been suggested for its adjustment in the light of post-war conditions and of long-term economic trends.

## PART I

## THE EFFECTS OF THE WAR ON JAPANESE FOREIGN TRADE[1]

### *The Situation at the Outbreak of War*

The outbreak of war—or rather the gradual development of the North China "incident," during the summer and fall of 1937, into an engagement of war proportions—did not come as an altogether sudden shock to an economy which had hitherto been functioning normally on a peace-time basis. On the contrary, ever since the Manchurian incident of 1931 the demands of the army and navy for "rearmament" had been forcing Japan in the direction of war-time economy. This was evident in the emphasis placed on the development of heavy industry, and in the gradual extension of state control over economic life. Especially in the last year preceding the Lukouchiao affair, intensified war preparations had made themselves felt with increasing force both in the field of domestic economy and in that of foreign trade. Thus when war came, its effect was not to alter the previous trend of economic development, but merely to speed up a process which was already well under way. Since July 1937 remarkable progress has been made toward the achievement of

[1] The following survey covers the period from the outbreak of the Sino-Japanese war in July 1937 to the outbreak of the European war in September 1939. It takes no account, therefore, of possible changes in the Japanese trade outlook as a result of the European hostilities. The situation in Europe is so uncertain at the moment of going to press (October 16, 1939) that no solid basis exists for speculation as to its economic repercussions in the Far East or elsewhere. It may be observed, however, that a prolonged war in Europe, toward which Japan remained neutral, would probably stimulate Japan's export trade in some degree, while at the same time increasing the cost of her imports. So long as Japan continues her military operations in China, there is little prospect that she would be able to repeat the enormous and profitable commercial gains which she achieved during the World War. See "Japan between Two Wars," *Far Eastern Survey*, October 25, 1939.

Most of the facts contained in this section are derived from current periodical literature, especially *The Oriental Economist*, the *Monthly Circular* of the Mitsubishi Economic Research Bureau, *The Japan Advertiser*, *The Japan Weekly Chronicle*, *The New York Times*, the *Monthly Return of the Foreign Trade of Japan*, and various bulletins of the United States Bureau of Foreign and Domestic Commerce.

a thorough military totalitarianism, although it cannot yet be said that this goal has been completely attained.

So far as foreign trade was concerned, the effects of mounting arms budgets, prior to the war, had been visible chiefly on the import side of the ledger. Imports of raw materials and capital goods for the expansion of heavy and military industry had since 1931 tended to counteract the influence of the rapid growth of exports which took place during the same period, thus keeping Japan's balance of merchandise trade on the passive side. During the latter part of 1936 and the winter and spring of 1937 there occurred an import boom of major proportions. Fear of inflation aroused by the record arms budget and the new cheap money policy induced a wave of speculative buying which was reinforced by the rising level of world prices. The import figures touched a high of ¥420 million in June 1937 (nearly twice the previous year's monthly average), and the excess of imports over exports for the first six months of 1937 was 126% greater than that for the same period of 1936.

In order to counteract the disturbing effects of this huge import movement both on the domestic economy and on Japan's international financial position, certain control measures were introduced which proved a foretaste of what was to come later. In particular, the licensing of exchange transactions was adopted in January 1937, though it was then described as a temporary measure. Notwithstanding the licensing system, pressure on the yen became so great a few months later that the decision was taken to resort to gold exports in order to maintain the position of the currency. Accordingly, in March 1937, the Bank of Japan began shipping gold for the first time since 1931.

The export trade, in the early months of 1937, was continuing the steady growth which had characterized it ever since 1931. In fact the tempo was somewhat quicker than it had been in the previous year. The most rapid advances over the depression low had of course taken place in 1932 and 1933, after which the rate of growth had steadily declined, falling to 8% in 1936. But in the first six months of 1937, exports gained 25% over the same period in the preceding year. Despite the rise of trade barriers abroad, Japan had held and even extended the markets won in the first years of the export boom. But the advantages of her trade gains were in part counterbalanced by the fact that, as the effects of currency depreciation wore off and world economy revived, the terms of trade had moved against her. In June 1937 the Mitsubishi index of export prices (December 10, 1931 = 100) was only 59% of the index of import prices. In 1931, of course, the terms of trade had been abnormally favorable to Japan, owing to the collapse of world raw material prices during the depression.

### External Factors Affecting Japanese Trade

Since the outbreak of hostilities Japanese economic life has been subjected to an increasingly drastic system of regulation for the purpose of mobilizing national resources for war-time needs. While these domestic controls have been the most important influence affecting trade development since July 1937, external factors have also been at work. Chief among these have been the general decline in world business conditions which set in about the middle of 1937, and the popular boycott against Japanese goods.

The effect of the business recession was, of course, to constrict the market for Japanese exports. Nor was Japan able to capture depression markets from other countries by offering extraordinarily cheap goods to impoverished consumers, as she had done in the post-1929 depression—partly because of rising costs and domestic restrictions hampering her export trade, and partly on account of the foreign trade barriers called forth by her previous exploits. On the contrary, during 1938 Japanese exports (outside the yen bloc) fell very much more rapidly than world exports in general, although they recovered somewhat in the early months of 1939, in sympathy with the world movement.

Partial compensation was afforded by the sharp decline in the prices of raw materials which accompanied the business recession, and which, as after 1929, worked to the advantage of countries like Japan which buy raw materials and process them for export. The extent to which the terms of trade have moved in favor of Japan is indicated by the fact that between June 1937 and July 1939 the ratio of export to import prices had advanced from 59 to 74. It is true that shortages and speculation created by import control at first raised the domestic prices of many articles far above their landed import cost, thus reducing the advantage to Japanese manufacturers of lower world prices. Price control measures may have subsequently eased the situation somewhat, but in any case this factor is discounted in the figures given above, which refer to domestic prices.

Another factor outside Japan's control and tending to reduce foreign demand for her products has been the boycott movement against Japanese goods. It is impossible to make an accurate estimate of the effectiveness of this movement, but available evidence indicates that it has played a substantial, though relatively minor, part in the decline of Japanese exports, at least in the first year of the war. The boycott has been especially effective in southeast Asia, where there is a large Chinese population many of whom occupy strategic positions in the wholesale and retail trade. In British Malaya, for example, where the organized movement has been strongest, imports from Japan declined by 74% in the first half of 1938, while imports from Europe gained 19%. Trade losses in southeast Asia during the first year of the war amounted to approximately ¥70 million, a considerable portion of which must be ascribed to the boycott.[2]

In the United States, Japan's chief market, a detailed study made for the American Council of the Institute of Pacific Relations demonstrates that the boycott movement, tying in neatly with "Buy American" slogans, has been fairly effective in regard to manufactured goods, though it has made little headway against silk, America's principal import from Japan. This study indicates that the trade loss sustained by Japan as a result of the boycott during the first twelve months of the war amounted to something on the order of $15 million (¥54 million), the remainder of the decline in imports from Japan—$38 million—being ascribed to other causes, chiefly the business recession.[3]

In general it may be said that the net effect of external influences on Japanese trade during the war period has been to aggravate, rather than to lighten, the burden of economic readjustments necessitated by the demands of the military campaign in China.

## Trade Control Measures

The economic problem faced by Japan was serious enough to tax the ingenuity of her statesmen to the utmost; and the crux of this problem lay in the field of foreign trade. For Japan is

[2] See *Far Eastern Survey*, Dec. 7, 1938, p. 284.

[3] See Nathan M. Becker, "The Anti-Japanese Boycott in the United States," *Far Eastern Survey*, Mar. 1, 1939; also Nov. 23, 1938, p. 270.

perhaps less able than any other great power to make war on her own resources. True, she is practically self-sufficient in foodstuffs, and under normal conditions very nearly so in essential manufactured products. But a large proportion of the raw materials necessary for the conduct of war, as well as for export industry, must be secured through the channels of international trade. Hence the efficiency of Japan's military operations in China, to say nothing of preparations for a wider conflict which is never absent from Japanese calculations, depended upon the extent to which skillful management could make up for her lack of strategic self-sufficiency.

With the realization that the conflict in China was one of major proportions, "expansion of national productivity" became the slogan of the day; or rather this slogan, familiar for several years past, was raised to a new peak of urgency. But however great zeal and efficiency might be displayed by Japanese industry, success in this endeavor depended upon the maintenance of imports of raw materials and capital goods in quantities sufficient to supply the demands of the armed forces for munitions and other supplies. Strenuous efforts were made to speed up the domestic production of primary products and to develop substitute materials, regardless of cost; but such measures could but partially relieve the dependence of military industry on foreign materials.

How are these to be paid for, in the face of declining receipts from both visible and invisible trade? Japan's liquid foreign assets had already been largely depleted in the pre-war years. She has been able to secure no substantial credits from abroad, although Germany has advanced considerable sums to Manchukuo. On the other hand, Japan has found it increasingly difficult to obtain ordinary short-term commercial credits; her purchases in the United States are now said to be conducted largely on a cash basis. Her gold reserves at the outbreak of war were not large, even when augmented by annual production in the empire, and prudence dictated that they be husbanded with the greatest care.

Japan has met this problem by applying a strict system of commodity rationing designed to ensure that her scanty supplies of foreign exchange should be expended only for such purposes as would directly or indirectly advance military ends. There are exceptions, of course; but broadly speaking, imports are permitted only for military use, for the munitions industries, or for export industries which will earn more foreign exchange. The brunt of this enforced economy is thus borne by those peace-time industries which supply the needs of the domestic population. These industries have been systematically deprived of imported materials; and even the favored industries find their supplies rigidly controlled, in order to keep the total imports within the limit of what can be paid for.

In order to attain these objectives, it has been necessary not only to regulate imports entering the country but to extend the rationing of materials into every department of national production and consumption. Price-fixing has also been extensively resorted to in order to counteract the effects of artificial shortages, plus inflationary government spending, on the price structure. As a corollary, new investment in peace-time branches has been forcibly discouraged. Thus, to a large extent, the whole elaborate apparatus of price, distribution and investment control which has grown up in the last two years has flowed as a natural and inevitable consequence from control of foreign trade, which is still, in practice, the principal pivot around which the system revolves.

In saying this there is no intention of implying that the recent intensification of state control over industry is merely a temporary phenomenon dictated by war conditions, or of minimizing the importance of militarist pressure to establish a totalitarian regime in which the interests of private capital would be subordinated to those of "national policy." Under actual war conditions the two motives—theoretical and practical—can hardly be distinguished, but there is no doubt that the necessities of war have powerfully strengthened the hands of Japanese-style "fascism." We shall return to this point later in discussing the possible long-term effects of the war upon Japan's place in international economic relations.

No attempt will be made here to describe Japan's system of war-time economic control in its entirety, but a brief account may be given of those features of it which directly affect foreign trade.[4] For most of the period under consideration these fall into two categories: regulation of dealings in gold and foreign

---

[4] For an account of accompanying measures in the field of domestic economy see G. C. Allen, *Japanese Industry: Its Recent Development and Present Condition,* Chap. V.

exchange, and direct regulation of import and export trade. The principal object in both cases, at first, was the control of imports; later, this motive was supplemented by a growing concern for restoration of the dwindling export trade.

Exchange control, as we have seen, dates back before the war —to 1932, in fact.[5] Following the gold embargo, certain regulations were adopted to prevent the flight of capital and excessive depreciation of the yen; they were not, however, intended to regulate the volume of foreign trade. The Capital Flight Prevention Law of 1932 was soon superseded by the Foreign Exchange Control Law of March 1933, which authorized the Ministry of Finance to restrict or prohibit certain classes of transactions in foreign exchange, including purchases of foreign securities, foreign loans, deposits, etc. Early in 1933 the yen was pegged at 1s. 2d. and no serious difficulty was experienced in maintaining its value until 1936, when, as pointed out above, fear of inflation became widespread as a result of the government's financial policies. In November 1936 the exchange regulations were revised with a view to ensuring that funds received in payment for export would be actually remitted to Japan. Down to the end of 1936, however, exchange control offered no impediment to ordinary commercial transactions.

The regulations announced on January 7, 1937, went much further and required a license for all purchases of foreign exchange, exceeding ¥30,000 monthly, in connection with payment for imported merchandise or letters of credit. This step was taken, as we have seen, in the midst of a speculative import boom which had created a heavy demand for foreign exchange. Its purpose was said to be merely to relieve the current pressure on the yen which was presumably of a temporary nature, rather than to exercise any permanent restriction on imports. Whatever may have been the intentions of the author of the measure, Finance Minister Baba, he was soon succeeded by Mr. Yuki, under whose regime the licensing system was applied in a fairly liberal manner. Although some control was exercised the heavy movement of imports continued through the spring, in fact down to the outbreak of the war, and the position of the yen was maintained by resorting, in March 1937, to a resumption of gold shipments.

The exchange regulations announced in January were sched-

[5] See "Foreign Exchange Control in Japan," *Oriental Economist,* October 1937.

uled to expire on July 31. Even before the commencement of hostilities in China, however, it had been decided to extend their duration and strengthen their provisions. On July 6, on the eve of the Lukouchiao incident, the monthly limit was lowered to ¥1,000 (reduced in December to ¥100), and permission was required for remittances for dividends or other profits, foreign obligations, patents or other industrial property, or for funds taken abroad by travelers. No further changes of consequence were made until a year later. In August 1938, however, the system was further strengthened by requiring that surpluses of foreign exchange be turned over by exchange banks to the Bank of Japan, which would regulate their distribution. While not providing for the complete centralization of foreign exchange dealings in the hands of a single agency, as has been done in some other countries, this measure was a step in that direction. Later certain other rules were announced, regulating brokers' activities, further limiting the export of Japanese or foreign currency, and lowering the free remittance limit to ¥100 annually.

Meanwhile the export of gold continued, and in September 1937—following the realization that the conflict in China was more than an incident—steps were taken to mobilize the nation's reserves of gold and foreign assets in defense of the yen. The Foreign Exchange Control Law was revised to confer on the government the power to mobilize and dispose of all foreign assets held by its nationals, should this become necessary.[6] Furthermore, Japan's gold reserves, which previously had been carried on the books at the pre-embargo valuation, were revalued to correspond approximately with their actual worth in terms of the depreciated yen. This resulted in a book profit with which, after the repayment of some old obligations, a Gold Fund Special Account of ¥747 million was set up. Some ¥450 million of this fund was utilized for the purchase of government bonds and Industrial Bank debentures, while the remainder was to be used as an exchange stabilization fund. While the hope was that the fund would operate merely to correct short-term fluctuations in the exchange market, pressure on the yen con-

[6] In April 1937, according to the *Oriental Economist*, such assets—Japanese obligations in foreign currency, foreign securities, foreign currency balances and foreign currency advances—amounted to some ¥1,476 million at face value, or approximately ¥2,761 million at current rates of valuation. This is presumably a gross figure, and not all such assets, of course, could readily be liquidated.

tinued to be so great that the original funds were exhausted in less than a year, and it became necessary to set up another "revolving" fund—described below in connection with the link system of import control.

After the war started it became necessary to exert a much more detailed and comprehensive control over foreign trade, both import and export, than had been possible under the exchange control regulations. The legal basis for this was provided by the Foreign Trade Control Law passed by the emergency session of the Diet in September 1937. Under this law the government was empowered to issue orders restricting the import or export of certain commodities or regulating their manufacture, distribution and consumption. The wide powers thus conferred extended far beyond the field of foreign trade proper, affecting the production, purchasing and marketing operations of every industry which either uses imported products or sells in the world market—which means almost every industry in Japan. Indeed, it was this law, rather than the much-publicized National Mobilization Act (passed in the spring of 1938 but even yet by no means completely enforced) which at first formed the backbone of the whole system of war-time control in Japan and still does so to a considerable extent.

Under the regulations issued in October 1937 to implement the Foreign Trade Control Act, as they were subsequently revised and extended, four classes of commodities were defined, subject to varying degrees of regulation in proportion to the urgency of the demand for them. Class A contained the leading raw materials of peace-time industry: cotton, wool, jute, wood pulp, wood, rubber, hides and leather. Imports of these commodities were subject to severe curtailment from normal levels. Class B listed nearly 300 articles of which imports were generally prohibited. These consisted for the most part of foodstuffs and manufactured goods which are of a non-essential or luxury character, or which can be manufactured in Japan—for example, beer, mineral water, watches, electric fans, tennis goods, woolen fabrics, gloves, boots and shoes. Class C contained two or three dozen articles considered essential for military purposes, exports of which were generally prohibited. These included rabbit fur, cotton waste, coal, fluorite, ores of antimony, tungsten and molybdenum, ferro-tungsten, iron pipes and tubes, special steels, antimony and sulphide of antimony, babbitt metal, automobiles and parts, and internal combustion engines. Class D, which was added later, specified a number of non-ferrous metals, imports of which were placed under supervision but given a preferential position. Commodities in this category include platinum, copper, lead, tin, zinc, mercury, antimony, sulphide of antimony, brass and bronze. It will be noted that no restrictions were placed on the importation of iron or iron ore, steel, oil or machinery, except in respect to licensing of foreign exchange.

The enforcement of these restrictions resulted in the creation of acute shortages of most imported raw materials, especially in the peace-time industries. Hence it became necessary to devise means of organizing the distribution of such materials among consuming industries as equitably as possible, and also to enforce the principle of giving preference in their allocation to military industry. To meet this need distribution control agencies were set up in most of the industries affected. The exact nature, functions and methods of these agencies vary with conditions in the particular industry and with the extent of government interest in it; moreover, the various schemes are constantly undergoing revision. In many cases some sort of industrial association already in existence took over the new duties; in others new agencies were set up, or old ones were reorganized or recombined. The functions of these organizations may include administration of a quota system for allocating and distributing supplies to the various factories, co-operative purchasing and marketing arrangements, control of prices, etc. The degree of governmental control also varies considerably. On the whole the tendency has been, so far as possible, to rely on voluntary action by trade associations rather than arbitrary control by the government; but the extent of direct governmental interference is increasing.

· Following is a partial list of leading commodities which have been brought under some form of distribution control: antimony, carbon black, coal, copper, cotton and manufactures, fertilizer, gasoline and heavy oil, hides and leather, iron and steel, lead, mercury, plantinum, rayon pulp, rubber, tin, wool and zinc.

The enforcement of import restrictions naturally led to a great deal of confusion and disturbance of ordinary business operations, especially in the peace-time industries, upon which the chief burden fell. The difficulties of doing business were increased by the fact that the import quotas were revised from time to time, so that the amount of imports of a given commodity which would be permitted in a given period was a matter of constant uncertainty; also by the fact that in order to import a consignment of goods it was necessary to secure licenses from both the Ministry of Finance (for purchase of foreign exchange) and the Ministry of Commerce and Industry, one of which might be granted while the other was refused.

Despite the drastic curtailment of raw material imports and attendant dislocation, the immediate effects on industrial production were not as serious as might have been expected, owing to the fact that unusually large stocks had been accumulated as a result of the heavy import movement in the first part of 1937. As 1938 wore on, however, complaints became increasingly frequent not only that the restrictions were hurting peacetime industry—which was regarded as inevitable—but that they were seriously embarrassing the export trade, thus defeating the very purpose for which they were intended, namely, the balancing of international accounts. Some relaxation was noted in the spring, but the situation remained unsatisfactory. As a result, during the summer of 1938—following the cabinet reorganization which placed Mr. Seihin Ikeda, a prominent business man and former managing head of the Mitsui interests, in charge of both finance and commerce ministries—the system of import and commodity control was subjected to an extensive overhauling.

The keynote of the new approach was the so-called link system, which had already been tried out on one or two commodities. Its purpose was to stimulate the export trade by freeing it from the difficulties which it had been meeting in securing raw materials. Precise details of the mechanism of the link system are difficult to obtain, and, moreover, the regulations vary from industry to industry and are subject to change. The principle, however, is clear: namely, that manufacturers are to be allowed to import linked raw materials in unlimited quantities, providing assurance is given that the corresponding finished goods will be exported to countries outside the yen bloc within a specified period. To finance such imports ¥300 million was taken out of the gold reserve and set up as a revolving fund, which began operations on August 1, 1938. At the same time the licensing of imports in Classes A and D (peace-time materials and metals) was abolished, regulation of such imports to be exercised henceforth through the single mechanism of exchange control.

Concurrently, the restrictions on domestic consumption were tightened up considerably, in order to prevent commodities imported for the use of military or export industry from being diverted into other channels. In June 1938 announcement was made that more drastic consumption restrictions would be imposed on a long list of commodities. This was subsequently implemented by orders regulating the industrial consumption of cotton, iron, rubber, tin, lead, antimony, zinc, nickel, certain hides and leathers, Oregon pine, machine tools, etc. In general the use of these materials in manufacturing for other than military or export purposes was prohibited except by permission of the prefectural governor, which it was understood would be granted only in special cases. In some instances the use of raw materials for the manufacture of specified articles considered non-essential was prohibited: for example, production of a variety of small iron articles, such as household utensils, was banned; tin, lead and antimony could not be used to make containers for toothpaste, toilet articles or foodstuffs. In principle, at least, exports to yen-bloc countries were put under the ban along with domestic consumption, since they yielded no foreign exchange.

An example of the methods of enforcement necessitated by this system is afforded by the case of cotton, the most important single industry affected, where the link system led to a complete reorganization of the structure of the industry. In this case the use of cotton in making goods for domestic consumption, other than military, was absolutely prohibited;[7] and at the same time all the previous control measures—raw cotton and yarn quotas, fixed prices, etc.—were abolished. Instead it was ordered that the manufacture of cotton textiles for export could be carried on only by members of the Japan Cotton Spinners' Association. The small weavers who had previously contributed largely to the export trade in textiles now had to carry on as jobbers for the big companies, or not at all. By thus centralizing cotton purchases it was hoped to check more effectively the bootlegging

[7] Recent reports indicate some relaxation of this ban in respect to certain articles such as workmen's clothing.

of cotton into forbidden channels. This measure thus affords a particularly clear example of the way in which war-time economic controls tend to foster monopoly by strengthening the position of large industrial units as against small ones and of trade associations as against outsiders, while at the same time bringing the monopolistic organs themselves under a greater degree of state control.

Although the link system is now regarded as the basis of import control in exporting industries, it has been applied only to a comparatively small number of commodities. These include, however, several of major importance. Its introduction has been gradual. As far back as October 1937 it was applied to imports of fragrant essential oils and tallow, which were linked with exports of soap. It was subsequently extended, the principle articles covered being the following:

| Link System Applied | Imported Commodities | Exported Commodities |
|---|---|---|
| October 1937 | Tallow, fragrant essential oils | Soap |
| January 1938 | Bristles, ebony, etc. | Brushes |
| January 1938 | Wood pulp | Staple fiber manufactures |
| March 1938 | Wool | Wool manufactures |
| May 1938 | Noil, etc. | Hats and hat bodies |
| June 1938 | Manila hemp | Japanese-style paper |
| July 1938 | Cotton | Cotton manufactures |
| August 1938 | Wood pulp | Rayon manufactures |
| March 1939 | Hides | Leather manufactures |
| March 1939 | Carpet wool and hair | Rugs |

The above items represented roughly 30 per cent of Japan's export trade in 1936. In addition, a different form of link system has been applied to a considerable number of less important export articles, the manufacture of which involves in each case the use of a variety of imported materials.

It is too early to pass final judgment on the success of the link system, which was widely hailed as the answer to the problem of import control hampering the export trade. Studying its effects in wool, where it has been in operation for more than a year, we find that wool imports increased immediately, then declined, then rose again in the spring of 1939, but only to one-third of their 1936 level. Exports of woolen textiles repeated the same curve a few months later, but failed to regain their normal level, much of the increase being in trade with yen-bloc countries. As regards cotton, where the system has been in operation since July 1, 1938, its effect on cotton imports has apparently been to stabilize them on a level around 50 per cent of normal. Exports of cotton goods, on the other hand, have increased considerably, and the gain has been almost entirely with foreign currency countries, as shipments to the yen bloc have been reduced to a mere trickle by the restrictions imposed against them in June 1938. Even so, cotton textile exports in January-July 1939 were somewhat less (in value) than those of the previous year. Rayon pulp imports declined steadily throughout 1938, notwithstanding the link system and the increased use of staple fiber, but rose sharply in the first months of 1939. So far as rayon textile exports are concerned, the effects of the link system, if any, are hard to discern. Total exports seem to have fallen slightly, the losses being entirely in non-yen-bloc trade.

An immediate result of the link system in the cotton trade was a decline in the unit value of exports, owing in part to a concentration by manufacturers on low-grade and unfinished goods where the turnover is more rapid. In wool and rayon, however, the introduction of the link system failed to interrupt a steady rise in unit value which had been in evidence for several years. This is another way of saying that in recent months the volume of cotton textile exports has risen faster than their value, while in the case of wool and rayon the reverse is true. Cotton goods, however, bulk far larger in the export trade.

Considerable dissatisfaction has been expressed in Japan over the working of the link system. It is as yet limited in scope and the difficult administrative problems which it involves have not yet been satisfactorily worked out. While application of the system to such simple and standardized products as textiles is relatively easy, much difficulty has been experienced in adapting the link principle to more complicated articles demanding a variety of raw materials. Efforts have been made to devise a "multiple link system" to take care of such industries, as yet apparently with little success. Even if successful, of course, the link system does not remove all of the factors which are impeding the export trade. On the whole, the evidence indicates that while the link system may be of some value in counteracting the impediments which war-time commodity control has placed in the way of Japanese export industries, it is unlikely to remove these difficulties entirely or to restore the export trade with non-yen-bloc countries to anything like its pre-war proportions.

The purpose of the link system was to enable Japan's export

industries to operate, so far as possible, on a normal basis in spite of war conditions. Other efforts to stimulate the export trade have also been of a generally orthodox character. There have been small appropriations to strengthen such activities as advertising and promotion, stationing more trade representatives abroad, market surveys, etc., and efforts have been made to cultivate new markets, for example in Scandinavia. In August 1938 the export indemnity system—originally adopted in 1930 to foster the development of new markets—was revised and extended. The government agreed to reimburse banks for losses sustained in financing export trade, up to a maximum of ¥4.7 million. But the serious decline of foreign trade has not yet led to any radical departures in export promotion policy, save for the link system, which as noted above represents an attempted return to normalcy rather than a break with recognized methods. Widespread demands for a new attack on the problem have led to the decision to establish a Ministry of Foreign Trade, but just what new methods this agency is expected to pursue is not yet clear.[8]

Deliberate depreciation of the yen has been rejected on the ground that it would raise the cost of imports and probably also induce retaliation abroad. Nor has Japan as yet resorted, on any large scale, to such elaborate expedients in the realm of barter, blocked accounts and currency juggling as those by which Germany has sought to maintain her exports in the face of similar difficulties. True, the principle of bilateral (or trilateral) trade balancing has for some years played an important part in Japan's commercial relations with many countries, notably Germany and Italy. But there has been no wide extension of this principle since the war started, though there has been talk of further barter arrangements.

Japan's situation differs from that of Germany in several respects. Her foreign debt is comparatively small, and service on it has been maintained, although restrictions have been

[8] Plans for the establishment of a Ministry of Trade met with at least a temporary setback when officials of the Foreign Office staged a "strike" early in October in protest against the cabinet's proposals. It was feared that centralization in the new ministry of responsibility for the conduct of foreign trade policy, hitherto divided among the ministries of foreign affairs, finance, and commerce and industry, would further reduce the role of the Foreign Office, whose prestige had already been seriously undermined by the events of recent years. Press Reports to date (October 16, 1939) state that the protest was largely successful, but details of the settlement have not yet been received.

placed on the remittance of profits abroad by foreign investors in Japan. She is thus comparatively free from the problem of foreign debt service which was one of the greatest weaknesses of Germany's international financial position; at the same time she lacks the weapon of frozen credits which Germany used to force exports to creditor countries. Moreover, a much larger proportion of Japan's foreign trade is with free exchange countries than was the case with Germany. In 1938, not more than 2 per cent or 3 per cent of Japan's exports were to countries having highly developed systems of exchange control (exclusive of the yen bloc); the British Empire and the United States and its possessions alone accounted for approximately 38 per cent.

## Effects on the Course of Trade

We may now survey the results of all these interacting and sometimes conflicting influences, domestic and external, as reflected in the development of Japanese foreign trade since the outbreak of hostilities. The most obvious consequence of the war has been a sharp drop in the value of both imports and exports, reversing the pre-war trend. In 1938, the value of exports was 15 per cent and that of imports 30 per cent below that of the previous year. The trend of monthly figures suggests that the severest losses thus far experienced were in the first six or eight months of the war. During most of 1938 both imports and exports followed their normal seasonal course, though at a level well below that of the previous year and, in fact, closely approximating that of 1936. Some improvement appeared in the first half of 1939, owing to improved business conditions abroad and partly, no doubt, to the link system. The quantum of exports has dropped somewhat more than their value, and that of imports somewhat less.

Overall figures, however, have very little meaning under present conditions. Much more significant is the striking shift in the geographical distribution of Japan's foreign trade which has taken place since July 1937. While trade with other parts of the world was declining, there was a rapid increase in trade with continental areas under Japanese control—now commonly, if loosely, referred to as the yen bloc (see Table 1).[9] Trade with

[9] The precise extent of the "yen bloc" is not easy to define, owing to the constant shifts in the boundaries of Chinese territory under Japanese military occupation, and the as yet very imperfect functioning of the measures by which

China suffered heavily in the latter part of 1937 in consequence of the hostilities in the north and at Shanghai. It recovered rapidly in 1938, however, especially in the north; while trade with South China, never large, practically disappeared for a time, but recovered after the occupation of Canton. By 1939, exports to China as a whole for the first six months of the year were 57 per cent above those for the last corresponding pre-war period, in 1937; imports, however, were still 5 per cent below those of 1937. Export and import trade with Manchuria had gained 95 per cent and 56 per cent respectively.[10]

With the yen bloc excluded, the decline of Japanese trade with the rest of the world becomes much more striking. In 1938, exports to the yen bloc increased over the previous year by 47 per cent, while other exports declined 36 per cent. Yen-bloc imports gained 26 per cent, others lost 37 per cent. In consequence, in 1938 no less than 43 per cent of Japan's total exports went to yen-bloc countries as compared with 24 per cent in 1936. The shift in imports was much less marked: from 14 per cent of the total in 1936 to 21 per cent in 1938. The same trend continued in the first six months of 1939, when the yen bloc accounted for 50 per cent of Japanese exports and 24 per cent of her imports.

This is not the place for a detailed discussion of the various measures taken by Japan to consolidate her economic position in North and Central China, which followed hard on the heels of military occupation. They have included the effort to introduce a new currency linked with the yen, tariff revisions by the Japanese-sponsored governments in Peiping and Nanking designed to favor Japanese trade, interference with foreign business and shipping, formation of more or less monopolistic agencies for trade and industrial development, etc. The mere presence of large numbers of Japanese troops and civilians in occupied China has in itself been a stimulus to Japanese exports.

Japan has sought to link the currency of these areas with her own. Technically, the Japanese consider that only Manchukuo and North China are so far included in the yen bloc. In this paper, however, the phrase is used loosely to designate areas in Manchuria and China under Japanese control; and for the purpose of statistical comparisons, all China is included as "yen bloc." This is not far from accurate as trade with unoccupied China practically disappeared soon after the outbreak of the war.

[10] The trade figures do not, of course, include military supplies shipped directly to the armies in China.

At the same time the speeding up of industrial development and exploitation of natural resources in Manchukuo, concurrently with similar efforts in Japan, acted as a stimulus to trade between the two countries.

We are more concerned here with determining the extent to which the increase in trade with Japanese-controlled areas has lessened Japan's dependence on the rest of the world for markets and raw materials. Analysis reveals that despite the rise in trade figures, Japan's net gains have so far been slight. Whatever prospects the future may hold, Japan's campaign in China has as yet achieved but little progress toward economic self-sufficiency, whether reckoned in terms of a peace or of a war economy.

There has certainly been a considerable expansion of markets, accompanied, however, by a more than counterbalancing decline in trade with other areas. In China, the gains have been largely in foodstuffs and textiles: wheat flour, fish, sake, canned goods, cotton and rayon manufactures. There has as yet been no heavy movement of capital goods for industrial development, although some increase is noted. Exports of consumption goods to Manchuria have also increased, but the bulk of the export rise in this case has consisted of capital goods—metals and their manufactures, especially machinery and instruments. It is clear that a large portion of Japan's exports to the yen bloc is made from imported raw materials. Hence, while they represent a welcome addition to business activity in Japan, their effect on the nation's international financial position is to this extent adverse rather than beneficial. In fact, as we have already seen, exports to the yen bloc have been placed under official restriction for this very reason, which has occasioned widespread dissatisfaction in Japanese business circles.

Thus the crux of the self-sufficiency question is in Japan's imports from the yen bloc rather than in her exports to it. Control of new territory is helpful in strengthening Japan's international financial position chiefly to the extent that imports from these regions can be made to take the place of imports from outside areas. And here Japan's success has so far been very limited. She is getting some cotton, wool, coal, iron ore, scrap iron, etc., from China, but not vastly more than she was getting before the war and not enough to reduce materially her dependence on other countries, particularly in view of the enlargement of demand in consequence of the hostilities. True,

the impounding of the Chinese customs receipts doubtless somewhat augmented her supplies of foreign exchange in the early
part of the war; now, however, it is improbable that any of these
payments are still being made in foreign currency. Likewise in
so far as Japan has been able to purchase supplies in China and
pay for them with fiat currency, and in so far as such supplies
replace imports, there may be a small gain. From the short-term
viewpoint, however—of immediate significance for its bearing
on Japan's ability to continue the war—it is probable that the
growth of trade with occupied territory has on balance weakened
rather than strengthened her economic position. Certainly it has
not strengthened it to an extent commensurate with the cost of
the undertaking.

Japan's apparent success in achieving an active balance of
trade in 1938 is thus seen to be illusory (see Table 2). Total
empire figures show that the large passive balance of the previous year—¥635 million—was replaced in 1938 by an active
balance of ¥60 million. But the passive balance with non-yen-
bloc countries—representing the actual deficit in foreign exchange—amounted to ¥624 million in 1938. True, this was a
considerable reduction from the ¥987 million of the previous
year, but it still represented a large debt item in the balance
of payments. In the first six months of 1939, the passive balance
excluding the yen bloc was about the same as in 1938.

Such adjustment of the trade balance as has been achieved
has come, as we have pointed out, entirely from the reduction
of imports. This reduction has not, however, been uniform;
the aim has been to maintain an uninterrupted flow of materials to war industry by dint of the strictest economy elsewhere. Although publication of detailed trade figures on
strategic commodities was suspended in August 1937, it is possible to get a general view of the drastic shifts which this system
of priorities has brought about in the composition of Japan's
import trade.

Such a picture is given in Table 3, depicting the trend in
several leading peace-time and war-time commodities. Of course
no such classification can be exact, since some petroleum, for
example, still finds its way into civilian consumption, and the
army uses some cotton and wool. It will be noted that even
imports of war materials declined slightly in 1938: in view of
the restrictions on civilian consumption, however, it may be

assumed that the supply to military industry was not correspondingly reduced. The most striking conclusion, however, is that whereas in 1936 the "war" group accounted for approximately one-fourth of Japan's total imports and the "peace" group for one-half, in 1938 these proportions were reversed. The increase in 1938 in oil and machinery is especially striking—reflecting, in the one case, either rapid consumption of petroleum products or the accumulation of reserves, and in the other, current efforts to enlarge the national productive capacity by plant expansion in munitions and heavy industry. The shortage both of finished goods for military consumption and of the means to produce them is also reflected in the pronounced shift in the distribution of imports by commodity groups which took place in 1938; the percentage of raw and semi-manufactured materials dropped from 82 to 75, while that of finished goods jumped from 11 to 17. In the first seven months of 1939, imports of war materials continued to rise, while imports of the peace-time materials listed remained about the same as in the previous year.

While these figures show clearly enough that the system of priorities in import control is working, it is impossible to judge whether or not it is working satisfactorily; that is, whether or not serious shortages exist in military industry. Statistics of production, stocks, etc., are no longer published for strategic commodities, nor would it be easy to estimate the demand. About the only evidence we have is indirect: the gradual tightening up of restrictions on non-military consumption of oil, coal, metals, etc. There have been reports that plant expansion in strategic industries singled out for state encouragement was being held up by inability to get permission to import machinery. Such incomplete evidence as we have points to a condition of increasing strain but not yet to one of desperation.

A similar conclusion is indicated by what limited evidence exists as to the condition of Japan's balance of payments. As pointed out above, the passive balance of merchandise trade with foreign-currency countries, though reduced in 1938, was still substantial. Shipping and other invisible receipts have undoubtedly suffered, though no figures are available. It may be remarked that in 1937 and 1938 gold exports were roughly equivalent to the deficit in merchandise trade, indicating that other items more or less balanced.

Perhaps the best index of Japan's present international financial position is afforded by an estimate, inexact though it must necessarily be, of her remaining gold reserves (see Table 4). This indicates that by October 1, 1939, Japan had exported a quantity of gold slightly in excess of her pre-war stocks. Meanwhile these stocks have been augmented by new production and the purchase of reclaimed gold, so that there remained on that date a gold reserve of something like ¥520 million,[11] plus an undetermined quantity of non-monetary gold and annual production probably around ¥200 million. This estimate, it should be emphasized, involves a good deal of guesswork, the relevant figures being no longer published in Japan. During nine months of 1939, monthly gold exports have averaged somewhat lower than in the corresponding period of 1938. Leaving scrap purchases out of account, and assuming that gold exports are continued at the same rate as in the first nine months of 1939 (allowing for a probable decrease in the latter part of the year owing to seasonal improvement in the trade balance), it might be concluded that Japan's gold reserves will be exhausted in a little more than a year. Should the trade balance improve in the meantime, either through a revival of exports or a reduction in imports, the date would be correspondingly postponed; should it deteriorate, by reason of foreign embargoes or otherwise, the date of exhaustion would be hastened. Even then Japan would not be completely bankrupt, for a totalitarian economy can carry on with little or no gold backing for its currency, and some imports over and above those paid for by exports could still be financed, though on a greatly reduced scale, from newly mined gold.

Such attempts at prophecy are rather pointless since there are too many imponderables involved. The war in Europe, for instance, may change the whole picture. The most that can be said is that Japan's financial position, though not yet desperate, is gradually growing weaker. Prior to the outbreak of war in Europe, it might have been said that if existing trends continued, the effect of commodity shortages on the efficiency of her armies and on the morale of her people seemed likely to become serious within a year and a half or two years.

---

[11] Of which the Bank of Japan reserve amounted to ¥501 million. At present these stocks are somewhat undervalued in terms of yen owing to the recent decline of the yen in sympathy with the pound sterling.

## Effects on Other Countries

A few words should be added concerning the effects of these rapid shifts in Japan's foreign trade upon the countries from which she buys and sells. Aside from the yen bloc, those nations whose exports to Japan consist mainly of peace-time materials— cotton, wool, etc.—have been badly hit. For example, imports from India declined by 62 per cent in 1938, from Australia 50 per cent, from Egypt 51 per cent and from South Africa 89 per cent. The large decline in imports from South Africa and the smaller loss sustained by Australia are largely explained by the fact that during 1937 Japan shifted her wool purchases toward South Africa as the result of a trade dispute with Australia, subsequently settled. Countries which furnish Japan with both peace-time and war-time materials have suffered less. Thus the United States, Japan's principal supplier, has lost only 28 per cent, the severe decline in cotton being partly offset by increased shipments of oil, machinery, etc. Similarly Netherlands India, which sends Japan oil as well as sugar and rubber, lost 42 per cent; the Straits Settlements, furnishing rubber, tin and iron, lost 20 per cent; while Canada, with wood pulp and metals as well as lumber and wheat among her principal exports to Japan, lost only 13 per cent. Japan's European partners fared much better, Germany losing only 3 per cent and Italy gaining 32 per cent. Japan's imports from Italy are still inconsiderable, but Germany now ranks third among Japan's suppliers.[12] Incidentally the relative gains made by Germany and Italy, especially the former, offer prima-facie evidence that in the allocation of exchange permits Japan has discriminated in favor of these countries.

Meanwhile the difficulties heaped upon Japan's export trade have proved boons to her competitors. Thus in southeast Asia, where Japan has suffered her heaviest export losses on account of the local Chinese boycott, European business has profited at her expense. Similarly the competitive position of American manufacturers has been strengthened in Latin America and the Philippines as well as in the home market; and there seems to have been some shift in American purchases toward Europe as well. Thus with minor exceptions the ghost of abnormal Japa-

[12] Trade with Germany, of course, has been largely cut off by the European war.

nese competition has been laid to rest, at least for the duration
of the war.

*Long-term Results of the War Affecting Japanese Foreign Trade*

While the subject of post-war adjustments in Japanese foreign trade is considered in the following section, it is proper
at this point to note certain conditioning factors which may be
expected as an aftermath of the hostilities. According to the
architects of the Japan-Manchukuo-China economic bloc, a
primary objective of the present war is to construct, on the basis
of Chinese resources and Japanese technology and enterprise, a
more or less self-sufficient integrated economy. Should this attempt be successful, the effects on Japan's position as a trading
nation would obviously be far-reaching. The more ambitious
projects call for Chinese cotton to replace American and Indian
in both Japanese and Chinese mills, Chinese iron to replace
Indian, Chinese wool to replace Australian, etc. Moreover, many
foreigners have expressed the fear that by utilizing Chinese resources and Chinese labor, which is even cheaper than Japanese,
Japan would be able to launch another drive on world markets
even more menacing to her competitors than that of 1932-7.

As we have seen, Japan is at present not much nearer the ac-
complishment of these objectives than she was at the beginning
of the war. There has been a considerable expansion of trade
with occupied areas but little concrete economic development
and little if any gain in self-sufficiency. This, of course, does not
prove that the idea of an economic bloc is essentially unrealiz-
able. Whether or not it is depends on the extent of China's
resources; on whether Japan can crush Chinese resistance and
restore peace and order in the occupied territory; on how much
capital can be raised either at home or abroad; and on the objectives and methods of Japanese developmental operations. The
answers to most of these questions remain in doubt at the present time, and it is not within the province of this study to discuss
in detail the prospects of Japanese-sponsored economic development in China. It may however be pointed out that in so far as
Japan is successful in achieving self-sufficiency through her own
efforts, the force of her claim to special international consideration in economic matters is proportionally diminished, while the
world trend toward forcing international trade into bilateral or
regional patterns is correspondingly strengthened.

While the post-war situation in China—whatever it may be—must be regarded as a primary factor conditioning the subsequent development of Japan's foreign trade and the possibilities of international adjustment, there are certain other conditioning factors arising out of the war which will make their influence felt whether the war ends in a Japanese victory or defeat. One of these is the violent distortion of the structure of Japanese industry which has been induced by the huge expenditure on armaments both before and during the war. The center of gravity is rapidly shifting from light to heavy industry.[13] Hence cessation of the present enormous demand for armaments would cause severe economic disturbance throughout the country. Such a situation, indeed, is the normal aftermath of war in any country, but in Japan the consequences of post-war deflation would in all probability be particularly severe. The usual difficulties arising from the collapse of a period of overexpansion and overcapitalization in industry would be aggravated by the inherent economic weakness of much of the newly developed heavy industry as well as of ersatz industries fostered by the war, which even in boom times depend heavily upon government subsidy and other forms of direct and indirect assistance. In addition, Japan is a country whose standard of living is so low that any considerable reduction might have serious social consequences.

The extremely grave problem which Japan will face in attempting to readjust her economic life to a peace-time basis is realized by many Japanese. Some of them entertain the hope that it will be possible to avoid or at least to cushion the shock by diverting the armaments industry into the manufacture of capital goods for export, mainly to China. The political uncertainties of the Chinese scene have already been alluded to. Without political control in China or extensive state subsidy at home, or both, Japan would be seriously handicapped in an effort to compete in the Chinese market for capital goods. This was made clear before the war, when Chinese purchases of railroad equipment, machinery, etc., were largely made in Europe and America. Besides, in order to keep her steel mills and foundries running, Japan would still have to import raw materials in large quantities from areas outside her currency system —at least for some time, until Chinese resources could be devel-

[13] See G. C. Allen, cited.

oped. The end of the war, therefore, would bring no immediate let-up in Japan's present economic difficulties; it might, indeed, intensify them. Even if Japan wins the war, and much more, of course, if she loses, it is difficult to see how anything except substantial foreign loans could stave off economic disturbances of the most serious character.

In view of the exigencies which Japan's economy must face even after the conclusion of hostilities, it is highly improbable that the elaborate system of state control over economic processes which has grown up during the war will be liquidated at its close. Certainly the present ruling groups are not likely to relax their vigilance, since in their eyes controlled economy is a matter of principle as well as of necessity. And even if reorganization of the government brought to the top a different set of interests, it is hard to see how any great liberalization of economic policy would be feasible in view of the economic difficulties which any post-war government would face. The most that could be expected for the immediate future would be that in a reorganized government more power would be wielded by commercial and financial groups who would use the mechanism of state control to promote their own interests rather than as an instrument of "national"—i.e., totalitarian-imperialist policy. Short of complete political and economic disintegration, however, it is very difficult to visualize anything in the nature of a genuine return to free competition, which under such circumstances would hardly be a beneficial event. If this assumption is correct, then controlled economy is one of the factors that must be taken into account in any attempt to formulate measures for the adjustment of Japanese trade after the war.

# PART II

## PROBLEMS OF POST-WAR ADJUSTMENT

The main facts concerning Japanese trade expansion prior to the present Sino-Japanese war, the international problems which it created, and the underlying economic factors involved, have been described and analyzed by various competent students. The space available here does not permit an exhaustive résumé of the findings of past research on the subject, nor does the scope of the present survey allow of detailed investigation into those aspects of the problem, practical or theoretical, which still require the elucidation of further original research. Our present purpose is rather to focus attention on the problem of Japanese foreign trade as it is likely to present itself in the post-war period.

In attempting to do this we are, of course, faced with a great uncertainty. We do not know what alterations in the political geography of Asia, the international balance of power, or the social and political structure of Japan and China the war may bring in its train, much less what the general configuration of international affairs may be at the time when the nations of the East turn to the task of reconstruction. Nor is it our purpose to speculate on these questions, absorbing and crucial though they may be. Our more limited object is, so far as can be done at this time, to single out the basic economic aspects of the problem as they are likely to present themselves in the immediate post-war period, emphasizing those which are likely to be operative regardless of the outcome of the war; and to suggest, on the basis of past experience, some of the techniques by which a practical solution might be sought in economic terms. It is for the statesman, not the economist, to weigh the results of economic analysis in terms of political desirability or expediency.

### Japan's Need for Trade Expansion

The dynamics of the problem of Japanese trade expansion lie within Japan herself; nor are they likely to be fundamentally

31

modified as a result of the war. The demographic, geographic and economic factors involved have been investigated with considerable thoroughness by both Japanese and Western scholars, and need be but briefly recapitulated here.

Japan's problem is only one of many confronting contemporary civilization as a result of nature's failure to arrange the populations and resources of the world to correspond with the twentieth-century system of competitive industrial capitalism operating within a framework of sovereign national states. Japan is one of the most densely populated countries in the world, though outranked by several. Comparisons with selected countries are given in the following table:

### POPULATION PER SQUARE KILOMETER[1]

| | | | |
|---|---|---|---|
| Japan | 169 | European Russia | 21 |
| Great Britain | 188 | United States | 16 |
| Germany | 137 | Java and Madura | 314 |
| Italy | 133 | Belgium | 270 |
| France | 76 | Netherlands | 233 |

Owing to the mountainous character of the Japanese islands, only about 15 per cent of the land area is cultivated, and not more than an additional 5 per cent is deemed capable of cultivation.[2] Hence the density of population in proportion to the cultivated area is particularly high in Japan: 11 per hectare as compared with 8.7 in the Netherlands, 8.2 in Switzerland, 5.0 in China, 4.9 in Java and Madura, 3.0 in Italy and 0.8 in the United States.[3]

Moreover the modernization of Japan has brought with it a rapid increase in population which is still going on, though it will not, experts believe, continue indefinitely. The present population is about 72 million. The intricate calculations of various students of demography, notably Professor T. Uyeda, lead to the conclusion that by 1960 Japan's population will probably have risen to about 80 or 90 million, after which it may become stationary. Even more significant from the economic point of view is the prediction, based on the existing age distribution, that from now until 1960 the population of working age will grow more rapidly than the total; or, to put it con-

---

[1] Ryoichi Ishii, *Population Pressure and Economic Life in Japan* (London, 1937), p. 63; F. V. Field (ed.), *Economic Handbook of the Pacific Area* (New York, 1934), p. 2.

[2] Field, cited, p. 65.

[3] Ishii, cited, p. 64; Field, cited, p. 56.

cretely, that in the next two decades the job-seeking population of Japan will increase at the rate of at least 400,000 a year.[4] From the population point of view, therefore, the most critical years for Japan are those that lie just ahead.

Owing to the scarcity of arable land, the growth of population in the modern era soon outstripped the possibilities of agricultural expansion. Hence Japanese agriculture is seriously over-manned, the average farm being only about 2.5 acres, and many families are forced to eke out a living through outside occupations. Even so only about half of the population is now engaged in agriculture, the remainder depending for their livelihood upon industry and trade. The farms, however, provide a permanent reservoir of cheap labor which keeps wage rates among the urban population at a low level.

Following the example of Great Britain and other densely populated countries, Japan has sought to provide employment for her surplus agricultural labor through the development of factory industry. Her rapid progress in this direction has formed one of the most dramatic chapters in modern economic history. But Japan's own territory does not and cannot provide either agricultural or mineral raw materials in anything like the quantities which her factories demand. While the Japanese Empire is largely self-sufficient in foodstuffs, it has been estimated (1933) that 27 per cent of the raw materials used in Japanese industry are imported. For many essential commodities the proportion is much higher: approximately 100 per cent for cotton, wool and rubber, 92 per cent for oil, 66 per cent for iron ore, 56 per cent for scrap iron, 25 per cent for pig iron, 10 per cent for steel, 18 per cent for coal (though coal is also exported), 95 per cent for lead, 44 per cent for aluminum, 45 per cent for zinc, 25 per cent for wood pulp. Nearly all of the tin, flax, jute, ramie, Manila hemp, and a considerable portion of the salt, antimony and many other materials of industry are imported.[5]

Imports, of course, must be paid for by exports; and in 1933 20.5 per cent of Japan's industrial production was exported, a

[4] Ishii, cited, pp. 126-37.

[5] Mitsubishi Economic Research Bureau, *Japanese Trade and Industry* (London, 1936), p. 493 and *passim*; Catherine Porter, "Mineral Deficiency versus Self-sufficiency in Japan," *Far Eastern Survey*, Jan. 15, 1936. Estimates are mostly for 1934 and 1935.

figure exceeded in 1929 (23.7 per cent) and probably also in later years. The ratio is similar to that obtaining in Great Britain, and considerably larger than that for the United States. Among individual industries, textiles depended on the foreign market to the extent of 35.1 per cent of total production in 1933 (raw silk, 78.5 per cent; cotton tissues, 54.4 per cent). The ratio for ceramics was 21.8 per cent, foodstuffs 11.4 per cent (canned goods, 75.3 per cent), chemicals 9.9 per cent, machinery and tools 9.3 per cent.[6]

While these estimates fall considerably short of accuracy the general picture which they present is not inaccurate. The conclusion is inevitable that Japan's position as a manufacturing nation is vitally dependent upon international trade.

This conclusion is supported by the weight of scientific opinion among serious students of Japanese economy, foreign as well as Japanese. For example:

. . . industry and commerce are the main channels into which additions to the working population tend to be drawn. Industrialization will have to be progressively extended in Japan in the near future . . . if the economic position of the Japanese people is to be maintained and improved, a still greater economic interdependence must develop between Japan and the rest of the world than exists now.—E. F. Penrose, *Population Theories and Their Application, with special reference to Japan* (Stanford University, 1934), p. 273.

. . . in view of her growing population and her shortage of industrial raw materials, a failure to expand the export trade must inevitably lead to a fall in the standard of life.—G. C. Allen, *Japan: The Hungry Guest* (New York, 1938), p. 253.

. . . we have been unable to escape the conclusion that if Japan is to increase, or even to maintain, her standard of life, she must direct a larger and larger proportion of her energies towards manufacturing industry in order to exchange her finished products on good terms for the raw materials of other lands. . . . Her problem will be to find markets for an increased volume of exports at prices which will not involve a deterioration of the conditions of her workers.—G. E. Hubbard, *Eastern Industrialization and Its Effect on the West* (London, 1935), pp. 154-5.

The major possibility for absorbing the increasing population, already destined to come into the labor markets in the years that lie ahead, is through further industrialization. . . . Japan's industrial future depends primarily upon the expansion of manufactured exports. . . .—Harold G. Moulton, *Japan: An Economic and Financial Appraisal* (Washington, 1931), pp. 399, 481.

Industrialization is more than a solution of the population problem. It is the key to the future of the country. . . . The progress of Japan's

[6] Mitsubishi Economic Research Bureau, cited, pp. 493-5.

industrialization depends very largely upon the country's ability to expand the foreign trade.—John E. Orchard, *Japan's Economic Position* (New York, 1930), pp. 48, 418.

There is, however, another school of thought, exemplified notably by Miss Freda Utley in her book, *Japan's Feet of Clay* (New York, 1937), which holds that the dependence of Japanese prosperity on foreign trade is greatly exaggerated. According to this view Japan has neglected to develop her domestic market. The plight of the farming population is due not to over-crowding but to an antiquated and essentially feudalistic rent system which keeps rural income at a subsistence level, and hampers the expansion of productivity through technological improvement. Furthermore, the cultivated area could be con-siderably enlarged and new crops such as fruit could be intro-duced if this were made an object of governmental policy. Likewise, it is held, the purchasing power of the urban worker could be greatly expanded if it were not for the control of in-dustry (and government) by a financial oligarchy which finds export trade based on exploited labor more profitable. Japan, it is claimed, must put her own house in order before she can demand special consideration from the outside world.

A recent book by a Japanese writer—*Population Pressure and Economic Life in Japan,* by Ryoichi Ishii (London, 1937)—while less sweeping in its conclusions, is notable for the emphasis laid on the need for considering domestic remedies for the problem of population pressure. "In a country such as Japan," Dr. Ishii writes, "where the natural resources are limited and the population density is high, special attention must be ac-corded to the creation of a well-balanced and a more or less equitable distribution of the national wealth." "It is generally conceded," he observes elsewhere, "that under the existing sys-tem of capitalism, which is an outgrowth of the institution of private property, the utilization of the economic resources of a nation may fall short of the possible physical maximum."[7]

There is little doubt that Japan's social and economic institu-tions, product as they are of a period of rapid and difficult transition from feudalism to industrial capitalism under stress of foreign pressure, leave much to be desired from the viewpoint of welfare economics. On the other hand, in reply to such

[7] Ishii, cited, pp. 247, 246.

criticism from foreigners Japan can quote to good effect the familiar maximum dedicated to the inhabitants of glass houses. Such exchanges of recriminations, however, are seldom conducive to the discovery of truth. A constructive approach will recognize that Japan's economic difficulties are rooted in both domestic and international conditions, and that a satisfactory solution can be found only by attacking the problem from both sides.

The present study deals with only one: the international. It would not seem unreasonable that foreign countries, before making trade concessions to Japan in the interests of international harmony and general prosperity, should require some assurance that such concessions will really serve the purpose for which they are demanded, namely, amelioration of the condition of the Japanese people as a whole. On the other hand, the view that Japan's difficulties are preponderantly of her own making must be rejected as being quite as one-sided as the opposite contention that they are principally the fault of international discrimination. The fact remains that no matter how perfect the distribution of wealth in Japan, no matter how efficiently her natural resources are utilized, she would still be unable to attain what is recognized as a civilized standard of living on the basis of her own resources alone. If her people are to wear cotton and woolen clothing she must import the cotton and wool; if they are to use automobiles she must import the iron, rubber and petroleum; and so on down a long list of consumption goods. These imports must be paid for by the export of Japanese products. For a country like Japan, no matter what social institutions she may devise, the international exchange of goods on a basis of comparative costs remains essential to her prosperity.

### How Much Is "Legitimate" Expansion?

Sober opinion in the West as well as in Japan is thus disposed to recognize the urgency of Japan's need to expand her foreign trade, and theoretically at least to concede, in the interests of general prosperity and peace, the legitimacy of her claim to increase her absolute and even her relative share of world trade. It is generally admitted, moreover, that while the advance of industrialization in any country inevitably brings some losses to competitors in older industrial nations, it also creates new demands for imported products; so that the ultimate result—at least under conditions of a relatively free international market —is a net expansion of trade in which other countries share, though perhaps not equally. This of course is particularly true of Japan because of her deficiency in domestic raw materials.

There is, however, a wide difference of opinion as to what constitutes a proper rate of trade expansion in the case of Japan, bearing in mind not only her legitimate claims but also the equally valid claims of other countries to protection of their national prosperity and standards of living. The matter of tempo is, indeed, the crux of the problem. This was brought out at the Yosemite Conference of the Institute of Pacific Relations in 1936, where it was

acknowledged by most that there was no real ground for complaining about Japan's expanding exports as such. They were recognized as a necessary outgrowth of Japan's increasing population, skill, and industrial organization. . . . Nor indeed was there objection to competition as such, but rather to the uncontrolled and disturbing manner in which it was allowed to make itself felt and to the unprecedented (and apparently unwarranted) speed at which Japanese exporters were dislocating western channels of trade.[8]

What, then, is the correct rate of expansion? From Japan's point of view it must be rapid enough to permit an increase in her industrial production sufficient to absorb the annual increment in her working population while at least maintaining, and preferably improving, the standard of living. From the point of view of other countries the rate must be slow enough to avoid sudden dislocation of established markets and to permit the necessary industrial readjustments abroad to be carried out in a gradual and orderly manner. Obviously it is not possible to reduce calculations of this sort to any statistical formula. The record of the past does, however, indicate that under favorable international conditions a practicable adjustment of the problem of tempo would not be necessarily unattainable.

In fact, during the decade following the World War it might be said that both of the conditions stated above were being actually realized in a reasonably satisfactory manner. The steady growth in Japan's population was accompanied by a much more rapid increase in the volume of her industrial production, which in turn was paralleled by the growth of foreign trade (see

[8] *Problems of the Pacific, 1936,* p. 64.

Tables 5, 6). Available evidence indicates that the Japanese standard of living was improving during the period, and Japan's increased exports were absorbed by world markets, if not entirely without friction, yet smoothly enough to create no acute disturbance or to provoke serious alarm. Fundamental to this happy state of affairs was, of course, the fact that the period was, until 1929, one of general prosperity and economic expansion throughout the world. Under such conditions Japan's gains excited relatively little comment, since they did not, on the whole, deprive her competitors of vital concrete advantages previously enjoyed. In 1929, indeed, a superficial observer might have concluded that the problems of readjustment raised by the industrialization of the Orient were working themselves out peacefully under the beneficent aegis of a relatively free international market.

This comforting illusion was rudely shattered by the events of the next ten years. The latent maladjustments which had underlain the "new era" of prosperity asserted themselves with terrifying force, and the next few years witnessed a violent contraction of world production and an even more severe shrinkage of world trade. It was precisely at this time that a more or less fortuitous combination of circumstances produced a sudden spurt in Japan's export trade, contrary to the declining world trend. Under such conditions it was not surprising that Japan's rapid advances in both old and new markets should have thrown her already harassed competitors into a state of acute alarm. Yet a broader view would have made clear that the combination of factors which produced the boom of 1932-7 was one which was not likely to recur and which was, by its very nature, necessarily of limited duration. Indeed, even before the interruption of the Sino-Japanese war the rate of export expansion in Japan had begun to slow down appreciably.

The boom of 1932-7 is generally considered to have been the product of four principal factors, of which only one—low money wages—was relatively constant. The second was the process of technological improvement and rationalization in Japanese industry and integration of her industrial and commercial organization which preceded and accompanied the trade boom. This process, actively fostered by both government and private interests during the previous period of depression, resulted in an increased productivity of Japanese labor and a heightened efficiency of her commercial organs. Further improvements of this nature, however, may be expected to take a more gradual course.

The third and probably the most important factor was the depreciation of the currency into which Japan was virtually forced by the disastrous consequences of resuming the gold standard in 1930 on the basis of an overvalued yen. Currency depreciation is a powerful stimulant for depressed exports, but it is generally conceded to be one whose efficacy wears off in the course of time. The fourth factor was the world depression itself, which for a time sharply lowered the prices of the raw materials purchased by Japan (thus counteracting the effect of a depreciated currency on the cost of imports), and at the same time reduced popular purchasing power in many of Japan's markets to a point where price rather than quality played the determining part in consumer choices. It may be added that it has never been established that export subsidies or dumping played any important part in the expansion of Japanese trade, particularly since the most flourishing export industries are those which receive little or no governmental support.

Despite the remarkable growth of Japan's export trade after 1931, the increase in her proportional share of world exports was very moderate, and was balanced, moreover, by a similar advance in her rank as an importer.[9] It was the concentration of her export gains in certain lines, particularly cotton textiles, that gave rise to the picture of Japanese goods driving others out of the market—which was true enough in some cases[10]—and led

[9] Between 1911-13 and 1932 Japan's share in world exports and imports, respectively, advanced from 1.4% to 3.2% and from 1.5% to 2.0%. Ishii, cited, p. 215. League figures, calculated on a slightly different basis, for the period since 1929 are as follows:

|  | Exports | Imports |
|---|---|---|
| 1929 | 2.94 | 2.80 |
| 1932 | 2.82 | 2.83 |
| 1936 | 3.59 | 3.53 |
| 1937 | 3.46 | 3.90 |

League of Nations, Review of World Trade, 1937 (Geneva, 1938), p. 25.

[10] Considerable detailed data on the effects of Japanese competition after 1931 may be found in the papers presented at the Sixth Conference of the Institute of Pacific Relations, Yosemite, 1936, especially G. E. Hubbard, Eastern Industrialization and Its Effect on the West (vol. 12); William W. Lockwood, Jr., Trade and Trade Rivalry between the United States and Japan (vol. 13); Les Conséquences du développement économique du Japon pour l'empire français (vol. 10), by M. A. Demangeon and others.

to the establishment of protective barriers of various kinds in other countries.

This was not, however, Japan's first encounter with foreign protectionism. As a relatively young industrial country, she has had from the beginning to dispose of her goods in competition with established interests in older countries whose home markets were heavily protected and which had already staked out for themselves most of the colonial markets of the world. Unlike her prototype, Great Britain, Japan "picked the wrong century" in which to industrialize. Especially since the World War, and more especially since the depression of 1929, the world-wide trend toward autarchy—inspired quite as much by political as by economic considerations—has steadily increased the difficulties of countries highly dependent upon export trade. It has borne with particular weight upon countries, like Japan, whose exports consist mainly of manufactured goods, which ordinarily can be more easily replaced by domestic goods than can basic raw materials.

Since 1931, most of the countries with which Japan trades have imposed additional import restrictions of one kind or another, many of them specifically directed against Japanese goods. Outstanding among these developments were the French quota system of 1932, which applied also to assimilated colonies including Indo-China; the Ottawa agreements of 1932, which provided for reciprocal preference among the countries of the British Commonwealth; the Chinese import tariff of 1933, which however was subsequently modified as a result of Japanese pressure; the Netherlands Indian Crisis Import Ordinance of 1933, under which quotas were applied to a large variety of commodities; the introduction of import quotas into the British crown colonies in 1934; exchange control and bilateral trade-balancing tariffs in Latin America; the textile import quotas in India, the United States and the Philippines, which however were arranged by agreement with Japan; and quotas or increased duties in Australia, Canada, New Zealand, Egypt and many other countries.[11]

These measures undoubtedly had the effect of checking the expansion of Japanese exports of the commodities affected, al-

[11] See Ethel B. Dietrich, "Closing Doors against Japan," *Far Eastern Survey,* Aug. 10, 1938; T. Uyeda, *The Recent Development of Japanese Foreign Trade* (I.P.R., Yosemite conference papers, vol. 7).

though the precise degree of influence which they exerted is impossible to estimate in view of the many other factors involved. For example, foreign barriers were doubtless largely responsible for the fact that cotton textile exports from Japan began to decline in 1936. At first Japan was able to compensate for such losses by increasing her exports of other articles, such as rayon and miscellaneous manufactures, and also by concentrating on new and relatively undeveloped markets. Thus despite foreign restrictions total Japanese exports, even with Manchukuo excluded, continued to expand until 1938, although at a somewhat slower rate than had characterized the first years of the boom. However, the long-run prospect was not too encouraging, as diversification of exports and of markets was almost certain to lead sooner or later to plugging of the remaining loopholes abroad. Whether or not the result of this process, had it not been interrupted by the war, would have been to check Japanese trade expansion altogether or to reduce its rate below that required by Japan's domestic necessities, it is impossible to determine. At least Japan had as much reason to fear economic encirclement as her competitors had to fear extinction by unrestricted Japanese competition.

But if, prior to the Sino-Japanese war, autarchic measures abroad were impeding or threatened to impede the maintenance of economic equilibrium and improvement of the standard of living in Japan, the achievement of these objects was also being impeded by certain aspects of Japan's own economic policy. Too much stress need not be laid on the fact that Japan is herself a highly protectionist nation, although many items of her tariff would be questionable on economic grounds in so far as they serve to foster industries in which Japan works under a demonstrable and permanent disadvantage. Of more immediate significance were the economic repercussions of Japan's continental policy, which were largely responsible for the fact that her astounding trade gains after 1931 did not bring with them a commensurate improvement in the conditions of livelihood of the Japanese people, save for certain favored groups. Not only were the profits accruing from foreign trade very unequally distributed, but a substantial part of the additional imports which export expansion made possible was diverted into the construction of a formidable body of armaments, which however, justifiable it may or may not have been on other grounds, must be considered almost a total loss from the economic point of view. Admitting that much of the new investment which took place in 1932-7 represented healthy industrial development, the fact remains that much of the expansion in heavy industry—which advanced much faster than light industry—was either economically unproductive or excessively costly. The imports necessitated by military expenditures go far to account for the passive balance of trade which prevailed during most of the period despite the growth of exports. Finally, in spite of this pressure the balance of goods and services remained active (see Table 7), and it was the export of capital to Manchukuo which weighed down the balance of payments and exhausted the bulk of Japan's foreign assets. Here again, while much of the investment in Manchukuo was of a productive nature (though the exaggerated tempo of development has been atacked on economic grounds), a considerable portion was directed toward strategic rather than economic advantage.

If, therefore, it is true that the benefits of expanding foreign trade as a solvent for Japan's economic difficulties have not kept pace with her needs in recent years, the reason is to be found partly in the policies of other governments, which under the influence of a vicious spiral of economic nationalism have erected ever higher barriers against Japanese exports, and partly in the policy of the Japanese government, which has diverted some of the gains of trade in non-economic directions. More important, however, than the policies of individual governments was the contraction of world economic activity during the depression, and the political tension which fostered an increasing tendency toward extreme national autarchy, both in Japan and in other countries. The problem of Japanese trade expansion, then, is one which cannot ultimately be solved piecemeal—a fact which should constantly be borne in mind when considering specific proposals for adjustment.

To return, however, to the question of how rapid a rate of export growth Japan would require in the future to provide employment for her increasing population. Speculation in such a field is not very fruitful, but a few rough calculations suggest that, given an expanding world economy, such expansion might be absorbed without undue strain. It may be pointed out that there have been two six-year periods since the World War during which the volume of Japanese exports doubled: the first in

1923-9 and the second in 1931-7. During the second period, which was one of severe depression in world economy, the growth of Japanese exports produced acute disturbance of world markets and serious friction between Japan and other countries. During the first, which was an era of economic expansion, a similar increase produced no such dire effects.

Japan's industrially occupied population was approximately 7,700,000 in 1937. Dr. Ishii tells us that at least 400,000 more workers will be coming into the labor market annually during the next twenty years. Let us assume that none of these additional workers is absorbed into agriculture. On the basis of the 1930 distribution of employment, we should expect 38 per cent of them to go into manufacturing industry and the remainder into commerce and other occupations. Since, however, commerce was seriously overcrowded in 1930, let us shift the ratio and call on industry to absorb 50 per cent of the new workers, or 200,000 per year. This would mean a gain of approximately 52 per cent in twenty years or 2.6 per cent per annum. This may be compared with the boom of 1932-7, when the index of employment rose by 57 per cent in five years, or about 11.4 per cent annually, while the average annual gain in volume of production was 18.1 per cent and in volume of exports 13.5 per cent (see Table 6). Of course this was an exceptional period, the previous years having witnessed a severe decline in employment, and the 1937 index represented a gain of only 17.3 per cent, or about 1.6 per cent annually, since 1926.

In estimating for a longer period many additional factors would have to be considered, including, on the one hand, a probable increase in the productivity of labor, and on the other, a possible decline in the ratio of production to exports owing to larger domestic consumption achieved through more equal distribution of the national income. It would appear, however, that during the 1932-7 boom Japan's industries were actually absorbing considerably more than the natural increase in the labor force (starting, of course, from a basis of severe underemployment), and that any failure to maintain internal economic stability during this period cannot be ascribed primarily to foreign trade restrictions; secondly, that given a proper internal adjustment, a less headlong rate of advance in production and exports would satisfy the needs of the expanding population; and thirdly, that export expansion pursued at a somewhat more moderate rate than that of the immediate pre-war years, and controlled to avoid excessive periodic booms and slumps, could be absorbed by world markets without undue dislocation, under conditions of an expanding world economy.

### Japan's Post-war Situation

Regardless of the outcome of the present Sino-Japanese hostilities, at their close Japan will be confronted by economic problems of the most serious and pressing character. The difficulties which she was already experiencing prior to the war, basic to which was the problem of maintaining social equilibrium, in the face of a growing population, through expansion and proper distribution of the national income, will be severely intensified by the losses and dislocations produced by the war. Conversely, the burden which any country must undergo in readapting its economic life from a war-time to a peace-time basis will be rendered more onerous by the underlying maladjustments present in Japanese society even before the war.

As pointed out in Part I above, Japan will enter the post-war period with an immense amount of her capital resources dissipated in warfare; she will probably have lost a large fraction of her foreign markets and all of her gold reserves and liquid assets abroad; her currency will at best be in a highly precarious condition; she will be saddled with an enormous national debt; she will inherit a huge incubus of newly developed heavy, military and ersatz industry, overcapitalized and much of it unprofitable under ordinary peace-time conditions; and her population will be impoverished by war-time taxation and inflation. Her nearest neighbor and best potential customer, China, will likewise be impoverished by the war and facing a gigantic task of economic reconstruction.

All of the above will hold true regardless of the terms of the post-war settlement. Obviously, however, the precise character of Japan's post-war problem, its degree of urgency, and the type of measures available for its solution, will be determined by the outcome of the conflict. Outstanding among Japan's announced war objectives is the creation of an "economic bloc" in Eastern Asia which will free her, at least partially, from the necessity of depending for markets and raw materials upon areas outside her own political control. In other words the war with China represents for Japan an attempt to solve her economic problems by unilateral action based on the principle of national or regional autarchy. To the extent that she is successful in this attempt, the alternative solution through measures of economic internationalism will be rendered both impossible and unnecessary. To the extent, however, that the attempt falls short of complete success—whether through the defeat of Japanese arms, or because of the inherent difficulties of developing a self-sufficient economic system on the basis of Chinese resources and labor and Japanese capital and technology—Japan will still find herself under the necessity of giving thought to her economic contacts with the rest of the world. Whatever the military outcome, it seems probable that the economic rehabilitation of both China and Japan will be long delayed unless substantial aid is forthcoming from abroad. Specifically Japan, whether victorious or defeated, will stand in need of foreign loans and of commercial arrangements favorable to immediate recovery of her export trade and to eventual repayment of her indebtedness.

It will clearly be to the advantage of foreign countries to provide Japan with such assistance as she may require in carrying out the task of post-war reconstruction, provided they have reason to believe that such action will serve to restore Japan as a prosperous client rather than a desperate competitor in world markets, and that support of Japan will conduce to general economic and political stability in the Far East. This raises important political questions as to the character of the post-war settlement and the nature of the Japanese government, discussion of which would lie outside the scope of the present memorandum. In the following pages we shall assume that the various questions outstanding at the close of the war, as between Japan, China and other powers, are settled in such a way as to raise no question of the political expediency of economic co-operation with Japan. If such an assumption is admittedly precarious, it is nevertheless the only one on which exploration of the possibilities of international collaboration for the solution of economic problems in the Pacific area can profitably be based.

## What Japan Has to Sell

Along what lines may post-war recovery in Japan's export trade be expected to develop? It seems unlikely that any sudden and striking changes are to be anticipated in the nature of the products in which Japan will be best fitted to compete in foreign markets. As in the past, her most promising opportunities will doubtless lie in textiles and miscellaneous light manufactures, chiefly though not entirely for the ultimate consumer (see Tables 8, 9, 10). Most economists who have surveyed Japan's economic situation have come to the conclusion that for greatest efficiency she should specialize in finished manufactures—particularly products demanding much labor and little capital for their fabrication—thus utilizing to the full the abundant labor supply which is her chief competitive advantage.

Certain trends toward modification of Japan's export trade which were evident before the war may, however, reasonably be projected into the future. Chief among these, perhaps, is the steady decline in the importance of raw silk, once Japan's leading export and still a major item. Silk is the only raw material which bulks large in Japan's export trade, and is exported in semi-manufactured form rather than as finished goods—which would be more profitable to Japan—largely because of the American tariff on silk manufactures. The sharp decline in the value of silk shipments after 1929 was chiefly due, it is true, to the depression in the United States, which takes the bulk of Japan's exports. But the increasingly severe competition of rayon, which has supplanted silk to the extent of more than four-fifths of the combined American consumption in 1938, is an ominous augury for the future. Even more depressing for the Japanese sericulturist is the recent announcement of nylon and other synthetic fibers which, it is claimed, will be able to compete successfully with silk in its last remaining stronghold—the full-fashioned hosiery trade—on both a price and a quality basis. Two plants for the manufacture of nylon are already under construction by the Du Pont Company in the United States, and if the claims made in its name are substantiated—as, in view of experience with rayon, there is no reason to think they will not be eventually—then in a few years Japan's silk trade may be reduced to a shadow of its former proportions. Such an event would necessitate drastic readjustments in Japanese rural economy and would render all the more imperative the development of new manufactured products for export.

During the recent trade boom cotton textiles displaced silk as Japan's leading export. In the cheaper grades, at least, Japan has enjoyed a competitive advantage which enabled her to undercut other exporting countries, notably Great Britain, and to capture a large share of the world market. In 1933 Japan first superseded Great Britain as the leading exporter of cotton textiles, and in 1938, despite the setback due to the war, she shipped 2,180 million square yards of cotton piece goods against Britain's 1,386 million. Japan has thus maintained her dominant position despite the fact that cotton goods have borne the brunt of foreign trade restrictions; but the effect of these limitations, together with the loss of the initial competitive advantage derived from currency depreciation, was seen as early as 1936 in a slight decline in both the volume and the value of cotton textile exports. Their ratio to total exports, which had advanced in the first years of the trade boom, fell back to less than the 1929 figure. Under favorable conditions Japan might maintain, and even temporarily expand, her exports of cotton textiles, especially if the pre-war trend toward greater emphasis on higher quality goods is continued. Cotton goods, however, are precisely the type of product which newly industrializing countries can most easily produce for themselves, and textile industries can be located without much regard to the availability of local raw materials, as Japan herself has demonstrated. In the long run, therefore, the international market for cotton goods seems bound to diminish as more and more countries come to manufacture their own requirements; and if some of them turn to exporting as well (as India and China have already done), with the advantage of labor costs as low or lower than Japan's own, the stress of international competition will greatly increase.

If the prospect for any considerable sustained improvement in Japan's two major exports, raw silk and cotton textiles, is somewhat unpromising, diversification of her export goods would seem to be imperative. The trend in this direction was in fact pronounced even before the war. The rise of woolen textiles to a position of prominence after 1931 was later overshadowed by the rapid growth of shipments of rayon yarn and textiles. The war itself has given a tremendous boost to the manufacture of staple fiber (used as a substitute for wool and cotton), which with the return of peace will doubtless be reflected in exports. There is also the possibility that Japan herself will develop other synthetic fibers, on the order of nylon, as substitutes for silk. In synthetic textiles she need have much less fear of competition from local products in colonial and semi-colonial markets, since the manufacture of chemical substitutes requires a heavy investment as well as a high degree of technical skill. While such countries may develop their own weaving industries they will probably need to import the necessary rayon yarn for a long time to come. It is true that these newer textile industries, unlike silk, require imported raw materials in large part. Japan, however, has a good deal of pulp-wood for paper and rayon and is experimenting busily and, it is claimed, with some success in the utilization of reeds, rice straw and other materials indigenous to Japan or Manchukuo.

Also prominent among Japan's newer export specialties are iron manufactures. These include small items of ironware for consumer use, such as cutlery and kitchen utensils; a much larger part, however, consists of machinery and semi-manufactured iron and steel products, that is, capital goods. Japan will have a special interest in promoting exports of this type after the war, in order to provide an outlet for the steel mills and machine shops which she has been building at high speed for military purposes. But—unless she is able to control a market in China and name her own price—she will be working at a heavy disadvantage owing to the high cost conditions under which her heavy industries operate (frequently necessitating a government subsidy in one form or another), as well as to their technical standards, which are still in many cases inferior to those of Europe and America. It is significant that, prior to the war, the bulk of her increasing exports of capital goods went to Manchuria, while the freely competitive Chinese market was supplied chiefly by Great Britain, Germany and the United States.

It seems inevitable that some part of Japan's overextended heavy industry will have to be liquidated if she is to return to a sound peace-time economy. On the other hand, it may reasonably be anticipated that between the huge requirements for physical reconstruction in China, and the urge in China and other "backward" countries to develop transportation, communications and manufacturing industries, the world and particularly the Asiatic market for capital goods should be large enough to provide elbow room for both Japan and the Western nations. Moreover, given political conditions favorable to economically sound planning and mutually advantageous collaboration, there would seem to be no reason why Chinese mineral resources and Japanese equipment and technical skill could not be co-ordinated to form the basis of an industry manufacturing at least the simpler forms of capital goods for the Asiatic market —a development which would contribute toward the solution of post-war economic problems in both countries.

Finally, recent years have seen a steady increase in both the volume and the diversity of trade in that large category of goods which can only be described as "miscellaneous manufactures." Bicycles, toys, electric light bulbs, brushes and hundreds of other light manufactures for the retail market, particularly those in which labor rather than materials and capital charges makes up the bulk of production costs, offer a promising field for further development—especially in colonial and semi-colonial markets where the process of shifting from handicraft to machine-made products is still going on. As these countries develop their own industries, however, Japan will find it necessary to shift her emphasis away from standard staples and to concentrate more of her energies on the production of specialties and quality goods; on mechanical gadgets such as cameras and electrical appliances, or luxury products such as textiles, clothing and sundry articles of use or adornment distinguished by their novelty, beauty or workmanship rather than by their cheapness. Such articles, indeed, unless international trade is cut down to bare necessities in the race for self-sufficiency, should command a market anywhere, even more in the advanced than in the colonial countries.

Meanwhile, although Japan will do well to specialize so far as she can on products for which raw materials can be obtained at home—such as silk manufactures (for which there will probably always be at least a luxury market), pottery and marine products—the limitations to such specialization are so great that any large expansion of her exports must inevitably involve, in the future as it has in the past, an expansion of her imports as well—especially minerals, textile materials and specialized manufactures, both capital goods and luxury items.

## Japan's Markets

There can be little doubt that in the immediate future Japan's most promising export markets will lie in those areas in which her recent trade expansion has been most rapid: namely, the colonial and other relatively unindustrialized sections of the world. Such countries, at least when prosperous, provide an expanding market for staple consumer goods which, as we have seen, Japan is particularly well fitted to supply. Furthermore, their populations, owing to low purchasing power, are more concerned with low prices than with high quality. By filling such a demand Japan has, it is generally conceded, contributed to the welfare of native populations, even though at the same time she has caused hardship to higher-cost competitors.[12]

It is true that with the gradual advance of industrialization in the hitherto relatively undeveloped countries of the world, these countries are likely to develop an increasing interest in tariff protection on their own account, and that in the course of time they will be able to manufacture for themselves many of the consumer goods which they now buy from Japan or elsewhere. On the other hand, if history is any guide, the process of industrialization itself tends to raise the standard of living, to create new demands and enlarge old ones, for both consumption and capital goods.[13]

On the basis of pre-war experience (see Tables 12, 13, 14), what are Japan's prospects in the various markets of the world?

*China.* The comparatively small volume of Japan's pre-war exports to China affords a clear example of the way in which essentially political factors can checkmate the operation of normal economic forces. China is a large and populous market, situated at Japan's door; a market whose demand for manufactured goods has been expanding under the impulse of westernizing influences, though such expansion was hindered by political instability, and whose special tastes Japan was particularly well fitted to supply. Yet between 1914 and 1936 the proportion of Japanese exports going to China fell from approximately one-fourth to one-twentieth, while Japan's share in China's import trade also declined. The development of large-scale smuggling operations and the fact that Manchukuo

[12] "When costs in the metropolitan country are relatively high, the inevitable result of protecting colonial markets for the mother country is to force up the colonial cost of living. . . . Thus the cost of promoting intra-imperial trade falls heavily on the colonies." Royal Institute of International Affairs, *The Colonial Problem* (London, 1937), pp. 311-12.

[13] "That colonial territories should advance to a fuller economic and political development is the avowed aim of most colonial powers who hold their empires 'in trust'; and that such development, however long it may take, will ultimately conduce to the material well-being of the world economy is at least promised by the present position of the United States, once colonial territory, but now a Great Power whose foreign trade in 1934 was almost as great as that of all the colonial territories of the world put together." *Ibid.*, p. 313.

has been excluded from Chinese statistics reduce the accuracy of statistical comparisons but do not alter the general observation that Japanese trade with China has failed to realize its possibilities, largely as a result of Chinese boycotts and other forms of discrimination for which the recurrent tension in the political relations of the two countries has been responsible.

A more specifically economic threat to Japanese export trade with China appeared on the horizon in 1929, when China assumed tariff autonomy. Four years later, the tariff revision of 1933 gave notice that she intended to use her newly won independence to take measures for the protection of her own infant industries, in accordance with the National Government's plan for far-reaching industrialization. The industrialization of China would inevitably mean a reduction of her purchases of imported textiles and other standard consumer goods, even though in the long run it might open up a greater market for capital goods, raw materials and more complex machine products—as has been true in the case of Japan. At any rate Japan strenuously and rather successfully resisted China's attempts to inaugurate a protective tariff, first by bringing pressure to bear to secure a reduction of rates on Japanese goods, and later by forcibly breaking down the tariff wall to permit large-scale smuggling in the north under Japanese protection.

In contrast to Japan's experience in China proper, the rapid growth of her trade with Manchukuo since 1931 shows how greatly Japanese exports to a section of China can be expanded when political factors are favorable rather than adverse. A large part of the export increase has been in capital goods for the development of Manchurian transportation, mining and manufacturing, financed by Japanese loans. Does the Manchurian experience furnish a reliable index to the prospects for economic intercourse with other parts, or indeed with all of China? To a certain extent, yes; but important reservations must be made. One is that the expansion of Japanese exports to Manchukuo has been possible only because of the complete control exercised by Japan over the Manchukuo government. Not only have the new construction projects in Manchuria resulted solely from Japanese initiative, but, as pointed out above, in a free market Japan would have had serious difficulty in competing in the sale of capital goods. Another reservation is that with her liquid capital already depleted by investment in Manchuria, by rearmament, and by the present war, it is highly improbable that Japan can by herself finance economic development in China on any such scale as in Manchukuo. Finally, Japan's efforts to develop the resources of Manchuria have proceeded at such an artificially forced pace, and with so much attention concentrated on strategic rather than purely economic objectives, that in the case of many of the new projects it is highly doubtful whether they would be sufficiently profitable to justify themselves in economic terms.

Nevertheless it remains true that China and Japan complement each other in many respects, and that there is no economic reason why trade between the two countries—in both directions—should not be capable of very great development to the mutual advantage of both. An analogy may be found in the case of the United States and Canada, where propinquity, similar tastes, political amity and a high standard of living in both countries have given rise to a large and flourishing trade between two neighboring nations in different stages of industrial development. Despite their very great similarity in resources and economic structure—much greater than between Japan and China—and despite the high protective tariffs on both sides of the border, the United States and Canada are among each other's best customers. Viewing the question of Sino-Japanese economic relations in the immediate setting of the post-war situation, it is obvious that the mere demand for physical reconstruction in China, aside from the potentialities of further industrialization, will offer an enormous market if China can secure goods on credit. In this market Japan may share. It would appear probable, however, that sound trade revival between Japan and China must proceed very slowly unless the requisite capital to finance Chinese imports, as well as to put the currencies of both countries on a stable basis, can be secured from the West.

*Colonial empires.* During the early years of her recent export boom Japan's most rapid advances, excluding Manchuria, were made in the colonial and semi-colonial markets of the world. In 1936 approximately one-fourth of her foreign trade, export and import, was with non-self-governing countries. In these regions, however, especially the imperial possessions of the great powers, she has encountered a formidable counter-attack in the form of trade restrictions calculated to preserve the colonial markets of metropolitan exporters. It was partly due to the general trend toward protectionism stimulated by the great depression, but partly also to the aggressive quality of Japan's attack on colonial markets, that in 1932-3 both Great Britain and the Netherlands abandoned their traditional policy of seeking no special preference in the markets of their own colonies.

British colonies—i.e., all parts of the British Empire not fully self-governing—accounted for something more than 17 per cent of Japan's total exports in the last pre-war year, 1936. While they are in various stages of industrialization, it is probable that for a long time to come most of the crown colonies will continue to figure in world economy primarily as producers of raw materials.

Prior to 1932 equal opportunity was the rule in British colonies. They had their own tariffs but instances of discrimination in favor of the mother country were exceptional. In 1932 Great Britain definitely swung over to protectionism at home, reversing the free trade policy which had prevailed since the middle of the nineteenth century, and simultaneously moved for a co-ordinated system of mutual preferences throughout the Empire, which was embodied in the Ottawa agreements of the following year. For the most part these preferences were secured by raising the existing tariff against foreign goods rather than by granting lower rates on British products. In 1934, as a direct result of the inroads of Japan into colonial markets, and after the breakdown of negotiations with Japan on the subject, a system of quotas was introduced throughout the British colonial empire (except where the conventional open door prevailed). First applied to cotton and rayon textiles, the quotas were subsequently extended to many other articles, and the effect was seriously to limit Japan's trade in the commodities affected.

India, Japan's second-largest market, is in a transitional state between colonial status and independence—both economically and politically. In contrast with the colonial empire, India has made considerable progress in the development of indigenous industries, especially textiles and iron, and her varied resources and large population give promise of the eventual achievement of a strong and well-rounded industrial structure. It is probable that such a development will increase rather than decrease her importance as a market for foreign manufactures.[14] In the meantime, however, the tendency toward protectionism appears to be increasing, while Great Britain still exercises sufficient influence over Indian tariff policy to secure imperial preference at many points, despite theoretical tariff autonomy.

Shortly after the World War, India abandoned the policy of a purely revenue tariff in favor of granting protection to specific industries, the number of which was gradually extended. As a result of Japanese competition after 1931, protective duties on cotton textiles were greatly increased while preferential rates were granted to British goods. By the Ottawa and subsequent agreements India granted further preferences in return for consideration given her own goods in British and colonial markets. Meanwhile the raising of duties on cotton textiles had precipitated a serious dispute with Japan, who retaliated by boycotting Indian raw cotton. The dispute was eventually settled, in 1934, by negotiation of an agreement whereby the Indian tariff on cotton textiles was reduced to 50 per cent and quotas were established for imports from Japan, their size being dependent on Japanese purchases of Indian cotton. It appears to have worked reasonably well, and was renewed in 1937 for three years. More recently the Anglo-Indian trade agreement of March 1939 granted greater preferences to British cotton goods while canceling the preferential treatment of a number of other products.[15]

The Dutch colonies, principally Netherlands India, rank next to the British as markets for Japan, taking 5 per cent of her exports in 1936. Here too Japan's rapid trade gains have been largely though not wholly responsible for the abandonment in 1933 of Holland's historic policy of the colonial open door, which had been maintained since 1872. The protection of native

[14] "To deduce from this evidence of increasing self-sufficiency a probable decline in the importance of India as a market for manufactures as a whole would be erroneous." G. E. Hubbard, cited, p. 295. Mr. Hubbard goes on to say that industrialization will increase the Indian demand for machinery and instruments, automobiles, chemicals, quality goods, and "the conventional necessities and luxuries of civilized life."

[15] The agreement was signed on March 20, 1939, after India had threatened to denounce the Ottawa agreement. It is to last for three years. India is to reduce her tariffs on British cotton textiles in the first year, after which the rate of duty will depend on British purchases of Indian cotton. She also grants a preferential duty on motorcycles. Indian preferential tariffs on rubber tires, hardware, tools, woolen yarns, cloth and knit goods, and other articles are abolished. *New York Times*, March 21, 1939.

industries, now being actively fostered in line with the colonial government's policy of diversifying the economic structure, has figured in this reversal as well as securing markets to the mother country. Under the Crisis Import Ordinance of 1933 and subsequent enactments, quotas or license systems have been applied to a large number of commodities. Negotiations with Japan with a view to bargaining for larger Japanese purchases of Netherlands Indian products were not successful.

American possessions took 2.4 per cent of Japan's exports in 1936, of which by far the greater part went to the Philippines and a smaller but not inconsiderable portion to Hawaii. Unlike Great Britain and the Netherlands, the United States never subscribed to the open door for its own possessions. The Philippines have their own tariff but their commerce with the United States is on a free-trade basis. Imports from Japan nevertheless increased rapidly after 1931. Japanese cotton textiles in particular offered severe competition with American goods, which was eventually regulated by an agreement of 1935 in which Japan agreed to limit her exports to a certain quota, while the United States promised not to raise the tariff. The agreement was renewed in 1937 and again in 1938 and 1939.

The prospects for future Japanese trade in the Philippines are affected by the uncertainty which still prevails concerning the relation of the Islands to the United States. Conceivably, a fully independent Philippines might welcome certain types, at least, of Japanese goods in preference to more expensive items from the United States, and might be disposed to grant concessions in return for securing a market in Japan for some of its own products. On the other hand, the Philippine government is trying hard, in the face of great obstacles, to develop light industries in the Islands in order to cut down their dependence on imported manufactures.

Owing to France's long-standing policy of substantially assimilating her colonies within her own high-tariff area, Japanese goods have made comparatively little headway in the French colonies. In 1936 they absorbed only 1.2 per cent of Japanese exports, of which two-thirds went to French Morocco, where the conventional open door prevails. In general, the colonies have been subject to the French import quota system first applied in 1932, and also to an exchange compensation tax affecting Japanese goods. In view of Indo-China's dependence on

Japan as a customer, and the fact that certain articles imported from Japan were not competitive with French goods, some concessions to Japanese products in that colony were granted by the commercial agreement of 1932. The prospects of extensive industrialization in Indo-China seem unimpressive in view of economic limitations and the reluctance of French business interests to encourage such development.

The other colonial areas of the world call for no detailed comment, being of much less importance, either actually or potentially, as Japanese markets. Of particular interest, however, are the special areas where maintenance of the open door is guaranteed by international treaty. The rapidity of Japan's trade gains in these areas, in contrast with the slower progress made in highly protected markets, shows what great possibilities for Japanese trade might exist were Japan able to compete in all colonial areas on an equal basis. For example, Japanese exports to French Indo-China increased from ¥1.7 million to ¥4.7 million between 1931 and 1936, while her exports to the free market of French Morocco rose from an amount so small that it was not separately recorded in 1931, to ¥20.5 million in 1936.

The open door is guaranteed in the Congo Basin under the treaty of Berlin (1885), the privileges of which were extended to Japan after the World War; in Morocco by the Act of Algeciras (1906); and in the A and B mandates to members of the League of Nations.[16] Whether Japan is entitled to claim the same privileges after her resignation from the League is a moot point.[17] However, areas where conventional equality of opportunity prevails are at present very limited.

*British Dominions.* The five British dominions, scattered in four continents, though closely linked with Great Britain, are fully self-governing countries. They are, in the main, producers of raw materials, though striving to develop domestic manufac-

---

[16] The conventional basin of the Congo covers an irregular strip across Africa, roughly from lat. 4° north to 12° south, and includes Kenya, Uganda, Ruanda-Urundi, Tanganyika, Portuguese East Africa, Nyasaland, the Belgian Congo, and parts of Italian Somaliland, Northern Rhodesia, Angola, French Equatorial Africa, the Cameroons, the Sudan and Abyssinia. See map in *The Colonial Problem*, cited, p. 50. The A mandates are Syria and Lebanon, Palestine and Transjordan; the B mandates are Ruanda and Urundi, Tanganyika, French Cameroons, British Cameroons, French Togoland and British Togoland.

[17] The United States, though not a member of the League, has obtained open-door privileges in the A and B mandates by special treaty. Quincy Wright, *Mandates under the League of Nations* (Chicago, 1930), p. 260.

tures. Together they absorbed 5.3 per cent of Japan's exports in 1936. They have fairly high protective tariffs, with preferential rates to some Empire goods under the Ottawa agreements.

Of greatest importance to Japan are Australia and New Zealand, which supply her with wool and other raw materials, while their propinquity and high standard of living make them excellent markets as well. Australia in particular has long been torn between the conflicting pulls of Great Britain and Japan in orienting her trade policy. Political loyalty and the importance of the British market incline her toward Great Britain, but the economic pull toward Japan is, or was before the Sino-Japanese war, very strong in the opposite direction. It has not, however, prevented serious trade disputes from arising. In 1936 Australia raised her duties on Japanese textiles, Japan retaliated by boycotting Australian wool, and after a lengthy trade war an agreement was reached in which Australia reduced her duties while Japan agreed to keep her export within an annual quota and to increase her purchases of Australian wool. The agreement was renewed in 1938 on terms somewhat less favorable to Australian wool producers. At present Japan is turning toward China and Australia toward the Empire. Under calmer political conditions a resumption of the economic rapprochement might be expected, although the growth of Australian industry indicates that if Australia loses interest in protecting British goods in her markets she may gain interest in protecting her own.

Canada likewise possesses an economy complementary in many respects to that of Japan, but her trade with Japan is less highly developed, owing partly to her very high tariff and partly to the counter-attraction of the United States. A brief trade war in 1935 resulted from Canada's imposition of exchange compensation duties on Japanese goods. After retaliations by Japan and counter-retaliations by Canada a compromise was reached, but the trade remained comparatively small, with the balance heavily in favor of Canada. South Africa has the distinction of being the only British dominion (except Eire, whose trade with Japan is minute) with which Japan had before the war a favorable balance of trade. Japan has done her best to meet this situation, in order to retain the South African market, by increasing her purchases of the more costly South African wool and other raw materials.

*Latin America.* The countries of Central and South America

constitute a market which Japan has only begun to develop. In 1931 they represented but 1.2 per cent of Japan's exports; by 1936, despite enormous percentage gains in some countries, they still accounted for only 4 per cent of the total. Most of these countries long ago achieved political independence, but their economic status has changed less rapidly. Like China, India and the Philippines, Latin America as a whole is in a transitional stage between an agricultural and a manufacturing economy, some countries, such as Brazil and Argentina, having made a great deal of progress, while others are still in the position of being largely suppliers of raw materials. Here Japan has to face, therefore, the protective tariffs of newly industrializing countries as well as the established position of the United States, and to a lesser extent of Great Britain, as suppliers to these markets. In addition many Latin American countries have in recent years been compelled to set up rigid systems of import and exchange control with a view to bilateral trade balancing. In an effort to meet this demand for reciprocity Japan has greatly enlarged her imports from Latin America since 1931. While many Latin American products, such as cotton and minerals, find a ready market in Japan, this is not true of other leading export commodities, notably coffee and sugar.

*United States.* Turning now to the advanced industrial countries, the United States demands first consideration. It is Japan's greatest single market, taking 22.1 per cent of her total exports in 1936. More than half of this consisted of raw silk, and a comparatively small proportion of directly competitive goods, owing to the extremely high American tariff on such products. As we have seen, however, the silk trade has been declining for many years, first in value and later in volume, and in view of newly developed substitutes the outlook is distinctly unpromising. Meanwhile the growth of sales of manufactured articles, though it has caused some disturbance in the American market for certain commodities, has failed to make up for the decline in export of silk. Japan's industrial expansion has, however, led to greatly increased purchases of American raw materials, among which cotton ranks first, and also of machinery and other capital goods. Thus since 1930 the balance of trade has turned in favor of the United States.

Japan's inroads into the American market have been met by tariff increases on comparatively few products. In the case of cotton goods, friction engendered by the rapid increase of imports from Japan was greatly allayed, if not entirely removed, by a voluntary quota agreement negotiated between private cotton textile interests in the United States and Japan. Under the agreement, concluded in 1937, Japanese manufacturers accepted a two-year quota in the American market; this was renewed for two years in January 1939. Similar quota agreements have been negotiated for several other products, including cotton rugs, velveteens and corduroys, and cotton hosiery.

The chances of Japan's making any really considerable headway in the American market depend to a very large extent on the tariff policy of the United States. Traditionally a highly protectionist country, the United States has under the Roosevelt administration been making a heroic and not entirely unsuccessful effort to take the lead in freeing the international market from the network of ultra-nationalist trade restrictions in which it has become entangled in recent years. No reciprocal trade agreement has, however, been concluded with Japan—partly because of the outcry over Japanese competition, and partly because of strained political relations between the two countries. It is true that by virtue of the most-favored-nation clause Japan has probably derived some slight benefit from the agreements concluded with other countries, despite efforts to narrow their application by minute definition of articles.

A reciprocal agreement with Japan has often been suggested, but no formal negotiations have ever been undertaken. The anticipated difficulties of making tariff reductions doubtless did not all lie on one side. Nevertheless the possibility is one that has yet to be thoroughly explored. Whether conditions will ever be favorable for such a step depends partly on whether the United States continues to adhere to its present liberal trade policy, and on whether the Pacific situation after the close of the present war is such as to bring an improvement in political relations between Japan and the United States.

*Europe.* European countries, although they are not commonly thought of as forming any considerable part of Japan's market, accounted for 11.4 per cent of her exports in 1936. About half of this went to Great Britain, most of the remainder being divided among France, Germany, Holland, Belgium, Sweden and Norway. It is thus the more highly industrialized countries of Europe with which Japan has been able to do the most business.

The foundations of Japanese trade with Great Britain were laid in the days when Britain was a free-trade country, and since the adoption of higher protective duties in 1932 the fact that the yen has been tied to sterling has undoubtedly facilitated commercial intercourse. Even so it is perhaps surprising to find that Great Britain buys as much from Japan as all of her dominions put together. Canned foods, silk and silk tissues are the leading exports among a long list in which both raw materials and manufactures figure prominently. Competitive products have encountered defensive measures in Britain as in other countries, while in a few cases the principle of voluntary quota limitations has received recognition.

Japanese exports to France have increased despite quotas and other barriers, and in the present year France has placed imports from Japan under a license system designed to redress the unfavorable balance of trade. Exports to Germany have been assisted by the tripartite trade agreements among Japan, Germany and Manchukuo, but remain small nevertheless. It will be noted that Japanese exports to eastern Europe are conspicuous by their insignificance, despite the appeal that Japanese goods might be expected to make in these predominantly agricultural countries. Excessive autarchic tariff policies, distance, and the inhibiting effects of exchange control and the barter system fostered by Germany, doubtless account for the comparative failure of Japanese salesmen in this part of the world.

Should Europe ever turn back toward more liberal exchange and tariff policies, some improvement in Japanese trade might be expected to result, particularly in eastern Europe. For Great Britain, the most promising line of attack seems to be in foodstuffs. Finally, in considering the possibilities of trade expansion both in Europe and in the United States, it would seem advisable for Japan to concentrate so far as possible on specialty and quality products catering to the luxury market, as France has done.

## Methods of Adjustment

The above sections have indicated that from the economic standpoint not only Japan but the world as a whole would benefit from the continuous and orderly expansion of Japan's foreign trade; and that the chances of realizing such expansion depend in large part upon reversal of the present trend toward increasing economic nationalism throughout the world, including Japan itself. Assuming such a reversal to be economically feasible and politically desirable, we may at this point examine some of the techniques of adjustment suggested or tried out in recent years which may be capable of application in the case of Japan.

It cannot be too strongly emphasized that, in the long run, the successful functioning of any techniques of commercial adjustment cannot be hopefully anticipated except under conditions of general and reasonably steady expansion in world production and trade. It has already been pointed out that the severe international disturbances caused by Japanese trade expansion in recent years arose in large part from the fact that Japanese trade was growing while that of most other countries was shrinking. The history of the past twenty years would indicate that the achievement of such a balanced expansion and the elimination of disastrous cyclical fluctuations call for far-reaching modifications in existing economic institutions and practices. The prescription of comprehensive remedies for the present ailments of world economy lies, fortunately, outside the scope of the present study. It may be recalled, however, that nearly all of the recommendations for world economic recovery which have been put forward by competent economists envisage as a principal plank the gradual removal of the more serious national barriers restricting the flow of international trade. It is the concrete application of this principle in the case of Japan with which we are concerned in the following pages.

A second and no less important preliminary consideration is the necessity of *controlled* expansion. It is not enough to level the dikes within which international trade is now confined, and then leave the stream to flow in what direction and at what velocity it will. No small part of the market dislocations and losses occasioned by Japan's recent trade gains has been due to the excessive speed with which Japanese goods, in some cases, practically swamped local markets abroad. Thus a shift which might have taken place with comparative smoothness had it been spread over a longer period proved a source of serious hardship when concentrated within a few short years. Japan, indeed, has on many occasions recognized the wisdom of making haste slowly by taking steps to curb the too rapid movement of her goods to foreign markets.

In the immediate post-war period, it is true, the paramount need is likely to be for stimulation rather than restraint of Japanese exports. Moreover, the spectacular quality of Japan's invasion of world markets after 1931 was due in large part to the temporary stimulus of currency depreciation, and is not to be regarded as indicative of the normal rate of advance of Japanese trade. Nevertheless, from a long-range point of view it is desirable to provide some sort of valve to regulate the flow of commerce in accordance with the expansion of Japan's productive powers and with the absorptive capacity of foreign markets at any given time. That this cannot safely be left to the operation of unregulated market forces, the experience of the last seven years would appear to demonstrate.

Fortunately a great deal of machinery capable of being adapted to such use already exists. Japan's manufacturers and traders are already highly organized in numerous trade associations possessing the requisite information, authority and experience to enforce a high degree of trade regulation. Furthermore, in all countries in recent years the state has tended to assume ever-widening powers of control over economic operations, and new organs and techniques have been devised for this purpose. This process has reached an advanced stage in Japan, but is by no means peculiar to that country. In too many instances such instruments of regulation, whether private or governmental, have been used for the purpose of enforcing curtailment rather than enlargement of production and trade. Yet to return to an era of unbridled competition—even if practically conceivable—would merely be to return to the beginning of a vicious circle. It remains to be seen whether capitalist instruments of control can be adapted to the aim of expansion of economic activity rather than "restraint of trade." This indeed is perhaps the outstanding economic problem of the twentieth century.[18]

[18] For an interesting and constructive discussion of "positive" and expansive as opposed to "defensive" and restrictive planning, and of the possibilities of such planning in a "mixed economy" where "free private enterprise and public planning work harmoniously side by side," see Eugene Staley, *World Economy in Transition* (American Coordinating Committee for International Studies, New York, 1939).

Professor Staley's book is one of the ablest examples of the constructive thinking which many economists and political scientists are now doing in an effort

If such an adaptation is possible it must, of course, cover many fields other than that of commercial policy in the narrow sense. It must include as a primary requisite some sort of international arrangement which will secure a fair degree of stability in the relations of the chief national currencies. It must provide for the regulation of international capital movements, coordinated with that of trade. In the case of certain key goods and services exchanged internationally, such as raw materials and shipping, special arrangements for the regulation of production and prices, the division of markets and the protection of consumer interests will doubtless be necessary. International controls must be accompanied by a sufficient degree of social control in domestic economic policies to permit a constant process of reallocating capital and labor and directing new investment in directions dictated by technological advances and by changes in the productive efficiency of different plants, industries and countries.[19] Above all, whether the agencies of control are national or international, public or private, loose or strict, their policies must embody, however flexibly applied, foresighted planning calculated to anticipate the "costs of progress" and to reduce them to a minimum by a continuous process of intelligent adaptation.

It is not proposed to pursue these points further in the present essay; but it should constantly be borne in mind that no

---

to bring the fruits of scholarship to bear on the practical problems confronting international society. Such studies demonstrate that the problem of drafting technical blueprints for a rational economic order, although extremely complex, is nevertheless not incapable of solution by the methods of the scientist. The problem of remodeling existing institutions in accordance with such blueprints, on the other hand, is a political one, to which as yet less attention has been devoted. Further investigation of the political dynamics of international economic reconstruction may necessitate some modification of the political assumptions commonly underlying such technical recommendations, including those in the present memorandum.

[19] "Positive planning must differ from restrictive planning in its attitude towards economic change. Instead of a defensive attempt to prevent new developments in other parts of the world from causing readjustments at home, it must seek to anticipate and smooth out the path of readjustment. . . . For example, if planning is directed to the defensive and restrictive end of maintaining the colonial market for an obsolescent British textile industry, a process of readjustment which ought to lead to better social use of resources is indefinitely postponed. Positive planning would meet the situation by allowing the production of textiles in Japan to increase, though not under the artificial stimulus of an extreme devaluation of the currency, and would replace some of Britain's textile production by production of machinery and other articles requiring a higher level of industrial skill and experience." *Ibid.,* pp. 284, 198.

mechanism devised for the expansion of international trade, however perfect, can be expected to function satisfactorily unless it is geared with other domestic and international policies adapted to the furtherance of the same end.

*Tariffs.* Tariffs are beyond doubt the oldest, most widespread and most effective obstacle that Japanese exports have to face. Even when, by their extraordinary cheapness, Japanese goods manage to surmount apparently unscalable tariff walls, this merely means that Japan is selling her wares on extremely unfavorable terms, with undesirable effects on her domestic economy and standard of living. That the present system of national tariffs, not excepting Japan's, is an economic monstrosity is generally admitted by students of international trade. However, tariffs exist, and as M. van Zeeland points out, these and other "measures of national protection were not resorted to lightly or frivolously, and if the countries protected by them still retain today the armor which they felt bound to put on, it is not without serious reason." A general international agreement, such as M. van Zeeland suggests, not to indulge in further tariff-boosting (save under exceptional circumstances) would be a step in the right direction which might conceivably find a part in some general international settlement embracing both political and economic questions. Any lowering of present tariffs, however, must probably come if at all very gradually and must proceed chiefly by means of reciprocal or regional arrangements.

*Reciprocal treaties.* Bilateral agreements for reduction of tariffs by the method of mutual concession are as old as tariffs themselves, and represent the most politically feasible method of effecting such reductions. Moreover, when accompanied by the unconditional most-favored-nation clause such agreements not only tend to increase trade between the two countries concerned but also, if practiced on a sufficiently wide scale, to effect a gradual lowering of the general level of tariff barriers.

The United States has recently pioneered in an attempt to bring about tariff reduction by reciprocal agreements. In principle concessions thus made are generalized to all countries, though in practice such generalization is greatly limited by careful definitions under the rule of granting benefits to the "chief supplier." Reciprocal agreements have been concluded with nineteen countries, not counting Czechoslovakia, and appear to have achieved demonstrable if necessarily limited success in their purpose of enlarging international trade. As already stated, the possibilities of a reciprocal agreement with Japan have been explored, but the idea has been abandoned for the time being, whether for economic or political reasons is not definitely known. Japan with her high protective tariff would doubtless find quite as much difficulty as any other country in granting tariff concessions—perhaps more than the average in view of the somewhat artificially promoted character of some of her protected industries. Nevertheless reciprocal agreements are one of the most promising means of enlarging trade between Japan and the United States, or between Japan and any other country. Most of Japan's present commercial treaties, it may be noted, contain the unconditional most-favored-nation clause.

*Quotas.* The import quota has been severely attacked as one of the most vicious impediments to international trade; it has also been defended as a less permanent and more flexible means of regulation than the tariff. In fact, it is a device which though frequently used to contract trade is capable of being adapted to its enlargement as well. Quota arrangements may be either unilateral or reciprocal, private or governmental. In most countries, import quotas have been imposed either as a quick and effective means of reducing total imports in order to protect the position of the national currency (as in France and Japan), or as an alternative to a high tariff for the protection of the domestic market in time of depression (as in the Netherlands).

In so far as import quotas have as their object the permanent reduction or limitation of imports, and in so far as they tend to freeze the shares of exporting countries in the trade of the given importing country, they obviously militate against the enlargement of international trade and against those natural secular shifts which are dictated by changing conditions of production in different countries. If, however, these dangers are recognized and avoided, the quota mechanism seems well adapted to the aim of regulating such secular shifts so as to avoid undue disturbance of markets, and especially of dealing with the problem of temporary adjustment to sudden and sporadic bursts of activity which would otherwise threaten market stability. It would seem possible to set up quota arrangements which would permit gradual increase as well as decreases, coupled with flexible administrative provisions which would permit a measure of national and international planning of the course of trade.

In such cases it would be desirable that the quotas be set up by negotiation and voluntarily accepted by Japan, and that they be subject to revision from time to time as conditions warranted. Japan's pre-war experience with negotiated quota agreements, while limited and by no means uniformly successful, suggests that the method is one deserving of further study. Japan has fully accepted the principle of voluntarily limiting the pace of her export expansion as one calculated to serve her own interests in the long run, and has in several instances undertaken herself to regulate the volume of her exports to an agreed annual quota. In some cases the *quid pro quo* was a reduction of the foreign tariff, or an agreement not to raise it further. In others the quota principle was made reciprocal, Japan receiving a higher quota than would otherwise have been granted in return for undertaking to purchase a given quantity of materials from the foreign country. Such an arrangement, of course, is possible only when a substantial trade in both directions is feasible, and is notably exemplified in the Japan-India agreement on cotton and cotton textiles.

It is to be noted that whereas this agreement, as well as the quota agreement with the United States on cotton textile imports into the Philippines and a number of others embodying the negotiated quota principle, were negotiated by the governments concerned, others—notably the cotton textile agreement for the United States market—were purely private arrangements between manufacturers' organizations, though concluded with the knowledge and approval of their governments. It should be added, of course, that tariff and quota bargaining can be combined in one agreement, as illustrated in the "tariff quota" whereby imports above a given quota are subjected to a higher tariff rate.

*Colonial open door.* Extension of the open door to all colonial territory has been suggested as a partial solution to the problems of "have-not" countries in so far as it concerns exports and access to raw materials. Proposals for opening colonial doors envisage action along one or both of two lines: gradual revision of existing discriminatory barriers by unilateral or bilateral action, or an international undertaking to secure equality of economic opportunity in all colonies not fully self-governing, by provisions similar to those now obtaining in the A and B mandates. Such proposals have much to recommend them in

view of the rather general admission that in many cases the
interests of colonial populations would be served by the removal
of artificial barriers which serve merely to raise their costs of
living while the advantages of protection all accrue to manufacturers in the mother country. It is true that colonies which now
enjoy, or may secure in the future, a degree of self-government,
might conceivably object to accepting an obligation not to practice discriminatory treatment; but this would not inhibit them
from imposing such protective tariffs as might conduce to the
development of their own local industries, so long as these applied equally to all countries including the mother country. The
alleged danger of flooding of colonial markets by Japanese goods
has been one of the principal arguments used against international action of this kind. In reply, it has been suggested that
sudden dislocation of trade might be avoided by regulatory
measures in which Japan herself might concur. Any general
agreement on the colonial open door would, of course, presup-
pose application to Japanese as well as to other colonies.

*Cartels.* Bilateral tariff or quota arrangements may in some
cases be impracticable or insufficient to deal with the problem
of competition in third markets, including the colonial. A possible method of meeting this problem would be through some
form of private or semi-governmental agreement based on the
principle of international cartel. This method of division of
markets has received little application in the Far East, although
there have been negotiations between Japanese producers and a
number of European cartels. In theory, a cartel arrangement
might be considered a logical solution for the problem of international cotton textile competition; but the practical difficulties
would be very great, owing to the decentralized organization of
that industry. The cartel idea should not be entirely ruled out,
however, particularly as applied to highly centralized industries
such as rayon and other chemicals, iron and steel, or aluminum
—with the important proviso that consumer interests be ade-
quately safeguarded. In the realm of raw materials, Japanese
adherence to the international sugar agreement would lessen
the difficulties of that harassed industry by removing the constant threat of uncontrolled production in Formosa. For the
hundreds of miscellaneous small manufactures which form so
large a part of Japan's export trade, however, the existing or-

ganization precludes the possibility of solving the problems of competition by negotiation between private producers.

*Barter agreements.* Japan has sought to expand her exports to many countries, notably in Latin America, by increasing her imports from them, and has likewise on occasion demanded that others buy more from her when the balance of trade was unfavorable. Reciprocal quota arrangements such as those with India and Australia also partake of the nature of barter although the conventional monetary mechanism is not discarded. Japan's principal experience with true barter agreements has been in the tripartite arrangements with Germany and Manchukuo, which have undoubtedly helped to stimulate trade among these three countries. The barter agreement is a device resorted to under stress of severe exchange difficulties when the ordinary mechanism of international transfers has broken down, and under more normal circumstances would be neither necessary nor desirable. So long as the exchange difficulties which brought it into being continue, it may be a useful means of permitting some international trade which otherwise could not be carried on. As a permanent measure, however, it is undesirable in that it is based on the principle of bilateral trade balancing, which coincides with that of economic advantage only occasionally and by chance.

*International consortiums.* Various devices have been suggested for the opening up of undeveloped territory, designed to make the open door effective in regard to investment and access to raw materials, as well as to export trade. Most of them are based on the principle of the international consortium or joint-stock company for developmental operations in Africa, Asia or elsewhere. Such large-scale operations, assuming they are directed toward economically productive ends, would be a useful means of increasing the world's wealth and at the same time of taking up the slack in capital goods industries the world over—not merely in Japan—which must be expected in event of a reduction in the present pressure for rearmament. These proposals also deserve close investigation, particularly as regards their possible application in China. They should not, however, be thought of merely as a scheme for amicable division among the great powers of opportunities for profitable investment and sale of capital goods. Unless due regard is given to the interests of the local populations affected, the economic, social and political consequences are likely to be unfortunate. "Exploitation," as the Royal Institute of International Affairs remarks, "is exploitation, whether by a single Power or a group of Powers."[20] Hence countries, such as China, which have reached a sufficiently advanced stage of civilization to assume the responsibility, should enjoy final control over the resources placed at their disposal; and in less advanced countries, the assumption of such responsibility should be considered the ultimate goal.

*Conclusion*

We conclude, in brief, that the special exigencies of Japan's economic situation, arising out of demographic and geographic factors beyond her own control, make the continuous expansion of her export and import trade for at least another generation an essential condition for the maintenance or improvement of the standard of living of her people, whatever form of social organization they may elect; that maintenance of such a standard is in the best interests not only of the Japanese people but of world society, partly because the enlargement of Japanese imports is advantageous to exporters in other countries, but more particularly because chronically depressed conditions in Japan would be a constant threat to the stability and prosperity of world economy and to the political equilibrium of the Far East. We do not assert that denial to Japan of legitimate opportunities for commercial expansion has been solely or even mainly responsible for such disturbances to international economic and political equilibrium as have in the past originated in Japan. We do assert that, in the post-war reconstruction period, the provision of such opportunities will be a necessary condition—though by no means the only one—for the maintenance of international prosperity and peace in the Pacific area and in the world.

We conclude, further, that there is no apparent reason why an expansion of Japanese foreign trade sufficient to make possible a balance between population and national income need

[20] *The Colonial Problem*, cited, p. 57. The point is amplified in a quotation from Leonard Barnes (*Peace and the Colonial Problem*, National Peace Council Conference, 1935, p. 33): "I quite see that development takes place by means of a merger of land and labour on the one hand with capital and technology on the other hand, and that the land and labour will be provided by Africans and the capital and technology by Europeans. But surely the object of the merger is to give Africa the mastery of the technology and the capital and not to give ourselves the mastery of their labour and their land."

cause serious maladjustments in other countries, provided it takes place in an orderly manner and under conditions of general expansion in world production and trade. There is, however, little ground for hoping that any satisfactory solution of the particular problem of Japanese trade expansion can be achieved except as part of a more comprehensive settlement of world economic problems, to which measures specifically dealing with Japan would contribute. We are convinced that a complete return to laissez-faire and the "automatic" mechanism of the market offers no hope of such a comprehensive solution. Hence if economic stability and orderly progress can be achieved within the capitalist framework, it must be by utilizing existing instruments of economic control, or devising new ones, for the purpose of promoting the *controlled expansion* of world production and trade.

This implies, in the first place, some measure of co-operative international regulation of currencies, capital movements, and exchange of goods and services, the nature and degree of regulation varying with the specific problem to be attacked. In the case of Japan, it implies particularly finding some means of reducing international trade barriers while retaining sufficient control over the flow of trade to provide a safeguard against the dangers of unregulated expansion. It implies, also, sufficient social control over domestic economic activity, in Japan and elsewhere, to ensure orderly readjustment to the shifts in the composition and direction of international trade which are inevitable, and indeed desirable, in a dynamic economy. It implies, finally, domestic policies calculated to distribute among the populations of the various countries as a whole, in a reasonably equitable manner, the benefits as well as any temporary losses ensuing from the enlargement of international trade.

Two further points may be noted. One is the preponderant share of Japanese trade—approximately 53 per cent of exports and 64 per cent of imports in the pre-war year 1936—which is conducted with the British Empire and the United States and its dependencies. This fact, together with the enormous weight exerted by the two great Anglo-Saxon communities in world commerce and in international finance, makes the policies adopted by them a decisive factor in determining the possibilities of any co-operative solution of the problem of Japanese trade expansion. The other point which deserves emphasis is the psychological, as distinct from the economic, effects in Japan of constantly rising foreign trade barriers. It is true that the "menace of economic encirclement" has frequently been much exaggerated by pressure groups in Japan seeking to justify nationalistic policies (as has the "menace of Japanese competition" in other countries). It is true, likewise, that when commercial negotiations are conducted in an atmosphere of mutual suspicion, substantial concessions may merely provoke dissatisfaction because they were not greater. It is equally true that when such negotiations can be carried on in an atmosphere of mutual confidence and constructive endeavor, even concessions of relatively small commercial value may produce a psychological effect out of proportion to their economic significance; they can, in other words, be used by pressure groups, if such exist, which are working for international co-operation.

In this memorandum we have attempted, in the interests of clarity, to deal with the problem of Japanese trade expansion in its purely economic aspects and to exclude political factors from the discussion so far as possible. We are, however, aware that in actuality economic and political factors are inextricably intermingled and mutually conditioned by one another. Hence if the problems analyzed above are to be discussed from the viewpoint of practical statesmanship, the relevant political factors neither can nor should be excluded from consideration.

It would transcend the scope of this paper to enter into a detailed discussion of such factors. This much, however, may be said. No measures of economic adjustment, however soundly conceived, can be expected to function satisfactorily save under conditions giving reasonable assurance of continued peace and security, both domestic and international. The record of history would indicate that such conditions are unlikely to result from a post-war settlement imposed by force by one nation or group of nations upon another.

TABLE 1

## JAPAN PROPER: TRADE WITH YEN BLOC AND OTHER COUNTRIES

(In million yen)

*EXPORTS*

|  | 1936 | | 1937 | | 1938 | | 1939 |
|---|---|---|---|---|---|---|---|
|  | First Half | Second Half | First Half | Second Half | First Half | Second Half | First Half |
| Manchukuo..... | 68.4 | 82.5 | 91.8 | 124.3 | 140.8 | 175.5 | 203.0 |
| Kwantung...... | 166.4 | 180.8 | 179.6 | 216.3 | 235.8 | 300.5 | 326.4 |
| Total Manchuria | 234.8 | 263.3 | 271.4 | 340.6 | 376.6 | 476.0 | 529.4 |
| North China.... | 26.1 | 34.0 | 47.1 | 34.7 | 82.2 | 116.4 | 124.1 |
| Central China... | 39.9 | 56.1 | 76.1 | 19.2 | 49.8 | 64.3 | 65.9 |
| South China.... | 1.5 | 2.0 | 1.8 | 0.4 | (*) | 0.2 | 5.7 |
| Total China.... | 67.5 | 92.1 | 125.0 | 54.3 | 132.0 | 180.9 | 195.8 |
| Total yen bloc... | 302.3 | 355.4 | 396.4 | 394.9 | 508.6 | 656.9 | 725.2 |
| Other.......... | 915.7 | 1,119.6 | 1,131.4 | 1,252.7 | 692.0 | 832.2 | 729.2 |
| Total exports.... | 1,218.0 | 1,475.0 | 1,527.8 | 1,647.6 | 1,200.6 | 1,489.1 | 1,454.4 |

*IMPORTS*

|  | 1936 | | 1937 | | 1938 | | 1939 |
|---|---|---|---|---|---|---|---|
|  | First Half | Second Half | First Half | Second Half | First Half | Second Half | First Half |
| Manchukuo..... | 123.0 | 82.6 | 140.6 | 108.5 | 199.9 | 139.2 | 225.5 |
| Kwantung...... | 16.4 | 17.4 | 23.5 | 21.7 | 32.1 | 28.2 | 31.3 |
| Total Manchuria | 139.4 | 100.0 | 164.1 | 130.2 | 232.0 | 167.4 | 256.8 |
| North China.... | 30.6 | 39.0 | 53.2 | 21.3 | 69.2 | 63.9 | 68.9 |
| Central China... | 29.6 | 43.1 | 38.9 | 13.8 | 9.7 | 17.9 | 28.0 |
| South China.... | 5.9 | 6.6 | 11.2 | 5.3 | 2.0 | 1.9 | 1.9 |
| Total China.... | 66.2 | 88.6 | 103.4 | 40.2 | 80.9 | 83.7 | 98.8 |
| Total yen bloc... | 205.6 | 188.6 | 267.5 | 170.4 | 312.9 | 251.1 | 355.6 |
| Other.......... | 1,284.2 | 1,085.3 | 1,878.4 | 1,466.9 | 1,081.6 | 1,017.7 | 1,122.7 |
| Total imports... | 1,498.8 | 1,273.9 | 2,145.9 | 1,637.3 | 1,394.5 | 1,268.8 | 1,478.3 |

* Less than ¥100,000.

## TABLE 2

### JAPANESE EMPIRE: TRADE WITH YEN BLOC AND OTHER COUNTRIES[1]

(In million yen)

| | Exports | | Imports | | Balance | |
|---|---|---|---|---|---|---|
| | 1937 | 1938 | 1937 | 1938 | 1937 | 1938 |
| Manchukuo and Kwantung.... | 710 | 1,013 | 388 | 493 | +322 | +520 |
| China...................... | 190 | 343 | 160 | 179 | + 30 | +164 |
| Total yen bloc............. | 900 | 1,356 | 548 | 672 | +352 | +684 |
| Other..................... | 2,418 | 1,539 | 3,405 | 2,163 | −987 | −624 |
| Total trade................ | 3,318 | 2,895 | 3,953 | 2,835 | −635 | + 60 |

[1] Excluding the South Sea islands (*Nanyo*), whose trade is negligible. Adapted from Mitsubishi Economic Research Bureau, *Monthly Circular*, April 1939.

## TABLE 3

### JAPAN: IMPORTS OF SELECTED WAR-TIME AND PEACE-TIME MATERIALS

(In million yen)

*War-time Materials*

| | 1936 | 1937 | 1938 | 1938 Jan.–July | 1939 Jan.–July |
|---|---|---|---|---|---|
| Ores and metals[1]............. | 375 | 901 | 662 | 389 | 484 |
| Oils, "other"[2]................ | 184 | 280 | 320 | 173 | 159 |
| Machinery[3].................. | 92 | 159 | 236 | 137 | 158 |
| Automobiles, etc.[4]............ | 44 | 58 | 62 | 48 | 16 |
| Total..................... | 695 | 1,398 | 1,280 | 747 | 817 |
| Per cent of total imports....... | 25 | 37 | 48 | 47 | 42 |

*Peace-time Materials*

| | 1936 | 1937 | 1938 | 1938 Jan.–July | 1939 Jan.–July |
|---|---|---|---|---|---|
| Raw cotton................... | 850 | 850 | 436 | 250 | 255 |
| Other vegetable fibers[5]........ | 37 | 41 | 27 | 14 | 20 |
| Wool........................ | 201 | 298 | 94 | 61 | 49 |
| Rubber...................... | 73 | 99 | 51 | 30 | 31 |
| Wood pulp.................. | 67 | 117 | 42 | 36 | 34 |
| Wood....................... | 56 | 65 | 28 | 14 | 18 |
| Total..................... | 1,284 | 1,470 | 678 | 405 | 407 |
| Per cent of total imports....... | 46 | 39 | 25 | 25 | 24 |

[1] Ores and semi-manufactures, including scrap iron.

[2] Including most petroleum products.

[3] Industrial machinery, not including radios, scientific instruments, etc.

[4] Category including several articles no longer separately listed, of which in 1936 the chief item was automobiles and parts; also firearms and steam vessels.

[5] Manila hemp, jute, ramie, etc.

TABLE 4

JAPAN: ESTIMATE OF GOLD SUPPLY[1]

(In million yen)

| | |
|---|---:|
| Monetary stocks in Empire, January 1, 1937 | 1,740 |
| Estimated mine output, Empire and Manchukuo, 1937 | 190 |
| Estimated mine output, Empire and Manchukuo, 1938 | 200 |
| Estimated mine output, Empire and Manchukuo, Jan.–Sept. 1939 | 150 |
| Estimated purchases of scrap, Jan. 1, 1937–Sept. 30, 1939 | 135 |
| Total supply | 2,415 |
| Exports, 1937 | 890 |
| Exports, 1938 | 595 |
| Exports, January–September 1939 | 410 |
| Total exports | 1,895 |
| Balance, October 1, 1939 | 520 |

[1] These figures are subject to considerable qualification. Those for the original monetary stocks and for exports are reasonably accurate; those for mine output are less reliable but probably close enough for practical purposes; those for purchases of scrap are sheer guesswork, based on unauthenticated and conflicting estimates. The present monetary stocks, estimated at ¥520 million, are somewhat undervalued in view of the recent depreciation of the yen. In addition there remains an undetermined quantity of non-monetary gold in Japan, which the government is now trying vigorously to mobilize.

TABLE 5

JAPAN PROPER: VALUE OF EXPORTS, IMPORTS AND BALANCE OF TRADE

(In million yen)

| | Exports | Imports | Balance | Oriental Economist Index (1913 = 100)[1] | |
| --- | --- | --- | --- | --- | --- |
| | | | | Exports | Imports |
| 1900................. | 204 | 287 | − 83 | 32.3 | 39.4 |
| 1901................. | 252 | 256 | − 3 | 39.9 | 35.1 |
| 1902................. | 258 | 272 | − 13 | 40.8 | 37.3 |
| 1903................. | 290 | 317 | − 28 | 46.6 | 40.6 |
| 1904................. | 319 | 371 | − 52 | 50.9 | 47.4 |
| 1905................. | 322 | 489 | −167 | 48.4 | 61.3 |
| 1906................. | 424 | 419 | + 5 | 62.8 | 51.4 |
| 1907................. | 432 | 494 | − 62 | 63.6 | 61.6 |
| 1908................. | 378 | 436 | − 58 | 56.4 | 52.8 |
| 1909................. | 413 | 394 | + 19 | 63.4 | 50.1 |
| 1910................. | 458 | 464 | − 6 | 70.8 | 62.4 |
| 1911................. | 447 | 514 | − 66 | 68.6 | 66.1 |
| 1912................. | 527 | 619 | − 92 | 82.0 | 82.6 |
| 1913................. | 632 | 729 | − 97 | 100.0 | 100.0 |
| 1914................. | 591 | 596 | − 5 | 93.6 | 83.4 |
| 1915................. | 708 | 532 | +176 | 104.8 | 75.0 |
| 1916................. | 1,127 | 756 | +371 | 153.5 | 102.3 |
| 1917................. | 1,603 | 1,036 | +567 | 216.6 | 143.3 |
| 1918................. | 1,962 | 1,668 | +294 | 265.2 | 232.6 |
| 1919................. | 2,099 | 2,173 | − 75 | 304.4 | 301.7 |
| 1920................. | 1,948 | 2,336 | −388 | 270.1 | 318.1 |
| 1921................. | 1,253 | 1,614 | −361 | 186.9 | 212.5 |
| 1922................. | 1,637 | 1,890 | −253 | 249.1 | 253.8 |
| 1923................. | 1,448 | 1,982 | −534 | 217.6 | 264.2 |
| 1924................. | 1,807 | 2,453 | −646 | 276.6 | 330.1 |
| 1925................. | 2,306 | 2,573 | −267 | 347.9 | 365.6 |
| 1926................. | 2,045 | 2,377 | −333 | 306.1 | 332.5 |
| 1927................. | 1,992 | 2,179 | −187 | 293.2 | 308.8 |
| 1928................. | 1,972 | 2,196 | −224 | 294.5 | 302.6 |
| 1929................. | 2,149 | 2,216 | − 68 | 320.4 | 302.6 |
| 1930................. | 1,470 | 1,546 | − 76 | 210.4 | 208.1 |
| 1931................. | 1,147 | 1,236 | − 89 | 164.5 | 167.0 |
| 1932................. | 1,410 | 1,431 | − 21 | 198.3 | 198.4 |
| 1933................. | 1,861 | 1,917 | − 56 | 254.0 | 271.8 |
| 1934................. | 2,172 | 2,283 | −111 | 284.5 | 323.8 |
| 1935................. | 2,499 | 2,472 | + 27 | | |
| 1936................. | 2,693 | 2,764 | − 71 | | |
| 1937................. | 3,175 | 3,783 | −608 | | |
| 1938................. | 2,690 | 2,663 | + 27 | | |
| Jan.–July 1937........ | 1,810 | 2,505 | −695 | | |
| Jan.–July 1938........ | 1,412 | 1,604 | −192 | | |
| Jan.–July 1939........ | 1,762 | 1,725 | + 37 | | |

[1] After 1902, this index is calculated on the basis of selected commodities rather than the total value of exports and imports.

TABLE 6

JAPAN: INDICES OF FOREIGN TRADE, INDUSTRIAL PRODUCTION, POPULATION AND EMPLOYMENT

| | Volume of Exports Oriental Economist (1928 = 100)¹ | Imports | Volume of Exports Yokohama Specie Bank (1928 = 100) | Imports | Volume of Production Oriental Economist (1928 = 100) | Volume of Production Oriental Economist (1931–3 = 100) | Population (1928 = 100) | Employment Bank of Japan (1928 = 100)² |
|---|---|---|---|---|---|---|---|---|
| 1913 | 54.3 | 52.6 | | | | | | |
| 1914 | 54.5 | 44.1 | | | | | | |
| 1915 | 61.5 | 43.0 | | | | | 85.0 | |
| 1916 | 70.8 | 47.7 | | | | | | |
| 1917 | 79.5 | 46.9 | | | | | | |
| 1918 | 79.5 | 55.3 | | | | | | |
| 1919 | 69.2 | 66.4 | | | 65 | | | |
| 1920 | 58.6 | 65.2 | | | 63 | | 90.2 | |
| 1921 | 55.1 | 68.6 | | | 62 | | 91.4 | |
| 1922 | 67.1 | 85.3 | | | 73 | | 93.9 | |
| 1923 | 55.3 | 84.1 | | | 77 | | 94.2 | |
| 1924 | 71.1 | 92.6 | | | 81 | | 95.2 | |
| 1925 | 86.2 | 91.6 | | | 85 | | 96.2 | |
| 1926 | 87.6 | 99.9 | | | 89 | | 96.6 | 110.7 |
| 1927 | 94.8 | 105.5 | | | 95 | | 98.7 | 105.0 |
| 1928 | 100.0 | 100.0 | 100.0 | 100.0 | 100 | | 100.0 | 100.0 |
| 1929 | 111.5 | 103.2 | 116.2 | 104.9 | 110 | | 101.3 | 100.9 |
| 1930 | 97.7 | 89.8 | 102.6 | 92.1 | 109 | 93.9 | 103.7 | 90.8 |
| 1931 | 102.2 | 101.3 | 105.7 | 102.1 | 108 | 91.2 | 105.3 | 82.5 |
| 1932 | 117.5 | 99.3 | 125.0 | 100.9 | 124 | 96.9 | 106.7 | 82.7 |
| 1933 | 124.2 | 105.5 | 138.2 | 104.7 | 148 | 111.9 | 108.2 | 90.7 |
| 1934 | 145.3 | 114.2 | 163.3 | 111.6 | 166 | 126.2 | 109.8 | 101.1 |
| 1935 | | | 185.4 | 116.9 | 192 | 139.3 | 111.6 | 110.6 |
| 1936 | | | 202.4 | 128.3 | 212 | 148.8 | 112.8 | 116.8 |
| 1937 | | | 210.8 | 136.5 | 238 | 167.3 | 114.7 | 129.9 |
| 1938 | | | 174.4 | 99.7 | | 172.3 | | 143.1 |

¹ Original base 1913.
² Original base 1926.

## TABLE 7

### JAPANESE EMPIRE: BALANCE OF INTERNATIONAL PAYMENTS[1]

(In million old gold U. S. dollars)

| | Goods, Services and Gold | | | | | | Capital Movements | | | Balance Due to Errors and Omissions |
|---|---|---|---|---|---|---|---|---|---|---|
| | Mer- chandise | Interest and Dividends | Other Services | Total Goods and Services | Gold | Total | Long- term | Short- term | Total | |
| 1927 | −134.1 | − 1.5 | + 68.7 | − 66.9 | + 17.0 | − 49.9 | − 59.8 | + 81.9 | + 22.1 | − 27.8 |
| 1928 | −150.1 | − 11.1 | + 81.1 | − 80.1 | − 0.2 | − 80.3 | + 24.7 | + 29.3 | + 54.0 | − 26.3 |
| 1929 | − 75.5 | − 9.1 | + 93.4 | + 8.8 | − 0.3 | + 8.5 | − 24.3 | − 1.9 | − 26.2 | − 17.7 |
| 1930 | − 76.4 | − 12.5 | + 75.4 | − 13.5 | +141.6 | +128.1 | − 45.4 | −100.5 | −145.9 | − 17.8 |
| 1931 | − 69.4 | − 11.5 | + 52.8 | − 28.1 | +189.6 | +161.5 | −114.2 | − 39.1 | −153.3 | + 8.2 |
| 1932 | − 16.0 | − 10.5 | + 38.7 | + 12.2 | + 31.5 | + 43.7 | − 47.2 | − 45.4 | − 92.6 | − 48.9 |
| 1933 | − 10.7 | − 10.7 | + 27.8 | + 6.4 | + 7.0 | + 13.4 | − 8.2 | − 41.3 | − 49.5 | − 36.1 |
| 1934 | − 12.5 | − 4.7 | + 28.3 | + 11.1 | — | + 11.1 | − 39.5 | + 16.7 | − 22.8 | − 11.7 |
| 1935 | + 24.1 | − 2.4 | + 31.1 | + 52.8 | — | + 52.8 | − 77.4 | + 14.1 | − 63.3 | − 10.5 |
| 1936 | − 16.0 | + 4.3 | + 34.2 | + 22.5 | — | + 22.5 | − 39.0 | − 7.3 | − 46.3 | − 23.8 |
| Total | −536.6 | − 69.7 | +531.5 | − 74.8 | +386.2 | +311.4 | −430.3 | − 93.5 | −523.8 | −212.4 |

[1] League of Nations, Statistical Year-Book, 1937–38.

### TABLE 8
## JAPAN PROPER: EXPORTS AND IMPORTS BY ECONOMIC CLASSES
(Per cent)

| | Exports | | | | Imports | | | |
|---|---|---|---|---|---|---|---|---|
| | Food, Drink and Tobacco | Raw Materials | Semi-Manufactures | Finished Manufactures | Food, Drink and Tobacco | Raw Materials | Semi-Manufactures | Finished Manufactures |
| 1900 | 11.1 | 13.6 | 43.8 | 27.8 | 18.1 | 28.0 | 20.2 | 32.1 |
| 1914 | 10.7 | 7.7 | 51.8 | 28.4 | 13.2 | 55.2 | 16.1 | 14.6 |
| 1919 | 7.1 | 5.2 | 43.1 | 42.9 | 16.2 | 50.3 | 20.8 | 12.0 |
| 1925 | 6.4 | 7.1 | 47.3 | 38.1 | 15.2 | 58.0 | 12.8 | 13.6 |
| 1929 | 7.6 | 4.2 | 42.0 | 44.5 | 12.2 | 55.3 | 16.1 | 15.6 |
| 1931 | 9.1 | 4.0 | 37.7 | 47.5 | 12.9 | 55.6 | 14.7 | 16.0 |
| 1936 | 7.6 | 4.7 | 26.6 | 58.1 | 8.7 | 62.9 | 17.2 | 10.6 |
| 1938 | 11.2 | 3.9 | 24.9 | 58.3 | 7.5 | 48.7 | 26.3 | 16.8 |

### TABLE 9
## JAPAN PROPER: LEADING EXPORT COMMODITIES, BY VALUE AND PER CENT OF TOTAL
(Values in million yen)

| | Raw Silk | | Cotton Tissues | | Rayon Tissues[1] | | Silk Tissues[1] | | Wool Tissues | |
|---|---|---|---|---|---|---|---|---|---|---|
| | Value | % | Value | % | Value | % | Value | % | Value | % |
| Av. 1910–14. | 152.1 | 28.7 | 26.9 | 5.1 | — | — | 34.1 | 6.4 | — | — |
| Av. 1915–19. | 325.5 | 21.7 | 148.8 | 10.0 | — | — | 87.3 | 5.8 | — | — |
| 1921........ | 417.1 | 33.3 | 203.7 | 16.2 | — | — | 89.9 | 7.2 | — | — |
| 1925........ | 879.7 | 38.1 | 432.8 | 18.8 | — | — | 117.0 | 5.1 | — | — |
| 1929........ | 781.0 | 36.3 | 412.7 | 19.2 | — | — | 150.0 | 7.0 | 4.2 | 0.2 |
| 1931........ | 355.4 | 31.0 | 198.7 | 17.3 | 39.7 | 3.5 | 43.1 | 3.8 | 1.4 | 0.1 |
| 1933........ | 390.9 | 21.0 | 383.2 | 20.6 | 77.4 | 4.2 | 63.5 | 3.4 | 12.4 | 0.7 |
| 1936........ | 392.8 | 14.6 | 483.6 | 17.9 | 149.2 | 5.5 | 68.0 | 2.5 | 46.0 | 1.7 |
| 1938........ | 364.1 | 13.5 | 404.2 | 15.0 | 115.8 | 4.3 | 49.4 | 1.8 | 46.8 | 1.7 |

| | Cotton Yarn | | Iron Mfrs.[2] | | Machinery | | Pottery | | Canned Goods | |
|---|---|---|---|---|---|---|---|---|---|---|
| | Value | % | Value | % | Value | % | Value | % | Value | % |
| Av. 1910–14. | 57.8 | 10.9 | 0.9 | 0.2 | 2.0 | 0.4 | 5.8 | 1.1 | 2.5 | 0.5 |
| Av. 1915–19. | 104.9 | 7.0 | 16.6 | 1.1 | 10.6 | 0.7 | 15.2 | 1.0 | 6.8 | 0.5 |
| 1921........ | 80.6 | 6.4 | 9.0 | 0.7 | 12.9 | 1.0 | 20.8 | 1.7 | 5.9 | 0.5 |
| 1925........ | 123.1 | 6.0 | 14.7 | 0.6 | 9.7 | 0.4 | 35.3 | 1.5 | 13.6 | 0.6 |
| 1929........ | 26.8 | 1.2 | 15.2 | 0.7 | 13.6 | 0.6 | 37.0 | 1.7 | 25.7 | 1.2 |
| 1931........ | 8.5 | 0.7 | 10.2 | 0.9 | 13.6 | 1.2 | 19.3 | 1.7 | 18.9 | 1.7 |
| 1933........ | 15.7 | 0.8 | 26.9 | 1.4 | 25.9 | 1.4 | 35.6 | 1.9 | 47.0 | 2.5 |
| 1936........ | 38.3 | 1.4 | 40.3 | 1.5 | 82.1 | 3.0 | 43.5 | 1.6 | 71.1 | 2.6 |
| 1938........ | 39.4 | 1.5 | 52.2 | 1.9 | 156.5 | 5.8 | 40.5 | 1.5 | 92.8 | 3.4 |

[1] Prior to 1931 rayon tissues included under silk tissues.
[2] Includes finished manufactures only, chiefly small wares.

TABLE 10

## JAPAN PROPER: PRINCIPAL EXPORTS IN 1936

(In million yen)

| | | | |
|---|---|---|---|
| Plants and animals.......... | 4.0 | Clothing and accessories..... | 181.2 |
| Grains, flours, etc........... | 29.9 | Undershirts and drawers... | 30.1 |
| Wheat flour.............. | 17.6 | Hats, etc., and hat bodies.. | 19.7 |
| Beans and peas........... | 7.1 | Rubber-soled boots and | |
| Beverages, comestibles and to- | | shoes ................. | 15.1 |
| bacco................ | 174.6 | Kimonos................. | 13.5 |
| Comestibles in tin and bottle | 71.1 | Hosiery................. | 12.7 |
| Aquatic products......... | 22.2 | Jewelry................. | 11.9 |
| Refined sugar............ | 21.0 | Buttons................. | 11.6 |
| Tea.................... | 13.1 | Sarongs................. | 8.0 |
| Alcoholic liquors......... | 10.3 | Shirts.................. | 6.6 |
| Vegetable isinglass........ | 5.6 | Paper, pulp and manufactures | 44.3 |
| Skins, hairs, etc............. | 23.5 | Paper................... | 27.5 |
| Bristles................. | 7.7 | Minerals and manufactures... | 23.9 |
| Furs................... | 6.0 | Coal................... | 10.4 |
| Oils, fats, etc.............. | 74.8 | Cement................. | 8.0 |
| Vegetable oils............ | 35.5 | Pottery, glass and manufac- | |
| Fish and animal oil....... | 10.2 | tures................. | 69.2 |
| Hardened oil............ | 10.0 | Pottery................. | 43.5 |
| Mineral oil.............. | 5.3 | Glass and manufactures.... | 25.6 |
| Drugs, chemicals, etc........ | 62.2 | Ores and metals............ | 103.1 |
| Dyes, pigments, etc.......... | 19.3 | Iron.................... | 76.4 |
| Synthetic dyes............ | 6.0 | Copper................. | 9.9 |
| Yarns, etc., and materials.... | 524.2 | Brass.................. | 6.7 |
| Raw silk................ | 392.8 | Metal manufactures......... | 76.5 |
| Cotton yarn.............. | 38.3 | Iron manufactures........ | 40.3 |
| Rayon.................. | 29.2 | Insulated electric wire..... | 13.7 |
| Woolen yarn............. | 15.3 | Nickeled metal manufac- | |
| Cotton waste............ | 14.9 | tures................. | 5.5 |
| Spun silk yarn........... | 7.3 | Clocks, instruments, machin- | |
| Tissues and manufactures.... | 864.6 | ery, etc................ | 174.5 |
| Cotton tissues............ | 483.6 | Machinery and parts...... | 82.1 |
| Rayon tissues............ | 149.2 | Bicycles and parts........ | 25.0 |
| Silk tissues.............. | 68.0 | Automobiles and parts..... | 17.4 |
| Woolen tissues........... | 46.0 | Railway cars and parts.... | 12.7 |
| Rags................... | 15.8 | Miscellaneous.............. | 161.8 |
| Handkerchiefs............ | 11.1 | Toys................... | 36.5 |
| Tablecloths.............. | 10.4 | Wood.................. | 24.7 |
| Carpets................. | 8.5 | Lamps and parts......... | 18.6 |
| Blankets................ | 7.8 | Fish meal............... | 7.4 |
| Cotton towels........... | 6.8 | Plaits.................. | 5.8 |
| | | Brushes................. | 5.6 |

Total including re-exports.... 2,693.0

## TABLE 11

### JAPAN PROPER: PRINCIPAL IMPORTS IN 1936

(In million yen)

| | | | |
|---|---:|---|---:|
| Plants and animals.......... | 2.2 | Clothing and accessories..... | 1.3 |
| Grains, flours, etc........... | 201.2 | Paper, pulp and manufactures | 88.5 |
| Beans and peas........... | 82.6 | Rayon pulp.............. | 44.2 |
| Oil seeds............... | 42.9 | Paper pulp.............. | 22.9 |
| Wheat................. | 33.7 | Printing paper........... | 10.2 |
| Corn.................... | 20.5 | Minerals and manufactures.. | 100.4 |
| Millet.................. | 8.0 | Coal................... | 50.9 |
| Rice and paddy.......... | 5.1 | Phosphorite.............. | 22.4 |
| Beverages, comestibles and to- | | Precious stones........... | 7.1 |
| bacco................. | 74.6 | Asbestos and manufactures. | 6.1 |
| Sugar.................. | 20.9 | Glass, etc................. | 4.5 |
| Salt.................... | 17.8 | Ores and metals............ | 374.9 |
| Leaf tobacco............ | 10.2 | Iron and steel............ | 192.0 |
| Meat................... | 9.1 | Scrap iron............. | 80.9 |
| Skins, hairs, etc., and mfrs.... | 47.3 | Pig iron.............. | 42.1 |
| Hides and skins........... | 24.4 | Sheets............... | 18.9 |
| Bristles................. | 6.5 | Ingots and slabs........ | 15.9 |
| Leather................ | 5.5 | Special steel........... | 7.3 |
| Oils, fats, etc.............. | 197.5 | Pipes and tubes........ | 6.9 |
| Mineral oil.............. | 182.8 | Iron ore................ | 40.0 |
| Vegetable oils........... | 7.4 | Copper................. | 36.2 |
| Drugs, chemicals, etc....... | 196.4 | Lead................... | 27.2 |
| Rubber................. | 73.0 | Zinc................... | 16.4 |
| Ammonium sulphate...... | 33.9 | Tin.................... | 15.1 |
| Chloride of potash....... | 10.6 | Aluminum.............. | 13.2 |
| Sulphate of potash....... | 9.4 | Nickel.................. | 8.5 |
| Nitrate of soda.......... | 7.2 | Metal manufactures........ | 10.6 |
| Dyes, pigments, etc.......... | 23.5 | Clocks, instruments, machin- | |
| Synthetic dyes............ | 11.4 | ery, etc................ | 153.1 |
| Yarns, etc., and materials.... | 1,109.5 | Machinery.............. | 91.2 |
| Raw cotton.............. | 849.6 | Automobiles and parts..... | 37.0 |
| Wool................... | 200.9 | Miscellaneous.............. | 139.1 |
| Manila hemp............ | 20.2 | Wood................... | 55.5 |
| Waste or old fibers........ | 8.1 | Oilcake................. | 35.8 |
| Jute................... | 7.7 | Fodder................. | 8.8 |
| Ramie................. | 5.5 | Wheat bran............. | 8.7 |
| Tissues and manufactures.... | 16.7 | | |
| Wool tissues............ | 9.7 | Total including re-imports... | 2,763.7 |

## TABLE 12

JAPAN PROPER: EXPORTS AND IMPORTS BY GEOGRAPHIC AREAS

(Per cent)

### EXPORTS

|  | Asia | Europe | North America | Central America[1] | South America | Africa | Oceania |
|---|---|---|---|---|---|---|---|
| 1900........ | 43.8 | 22.1 | 28.5 | [2] | [2] | 0.2[3] | 2.2 |
| 1914........ | 46.9 | 15.5 | 34.1 | [2] | 0.1 | 0.4 | 2.9 |
| 1919........ | 45.5 | 9.3 | 40.8[4] | [4] | 1.0 | 1.2 | 2.2 |
| 1925........ | 43.4 | 6.6 | 44.8[4] | [4] | 0.7 | 1.8 | 2.6 |
| 1929........ | 42.6 | 6.8 | 44.1[4] | [4] | 1.1 | 2.8 | 2.5 |
| 1931........ | 44.0 | 9.1 | 38.3 | 0.3 | 0.9 | 5.1 | 2.3 |
| 1936........ | 50.9 | 11.4 | 22.6 | 1.5 | 2.5 | 7.3 | 3.6 |
| 1938........ | 61.9 | 9.7 | 16.3 | 1.1 | 2.2 | 5.1 | 3.5 |

### IMPORTS

|  | Asia | Europe | North America | Central America[1] | South America | Africa | Oceania |
|---|---|---|---|---|---|---|---|
| 1900........ | 30.2 | 45.5 | 22.7 | [2] | [2] | 0.5 | 0.9 |
| 1914........ | 51.1 | 26.6 | 16.4 | [2] | 0.4 | 1.1 | 2.4 |
| 1919........ | 49.4 | 7.4 | 35.6[4] | [4] | 0.9 | 2.5 | 3.1 |
| 1925........ | 47.2 | 17.4 | 27.4[4] | [4] | 0.3 | 1.6 | 6.0 |
| 1929........ | 38.7 | 18.9 | 32.7[4] | [4] | 0.7 | 1.9 | 6.3 |
| 1931........ | 40.0 | 16.2 | 30.6 | [2] | 0.6 | 1.5 | 9.5 |
| 1936........ | 38.4 | 11.9 | 33.3 | 0.8 | 4.1 | 3.9 | 7.6 |
| 1938........ | 38.4 | 14.1 | 37.8 | 0.3 | 3.4 | 2.2 | 3.6 |

[1] Includes Mexico and West Indies.
[2] Less than 0.1 per cent.
[3] Egypt only.
[4] Central America included in North America.

## TABLE 13

### JAPAN: EXPORTS TO SELECTED COUNTRIES

(In million yen and as per cent of total)

|  | China | | Manchukuo | | Kwantung | | Hongkong | | United States | |
|---|---|---|---|---|---|---|---|---|---|---|
|  | Amount | Per Cent | Amount | Per Cent | Amount | Per Cent | Amount | Per Cent | Amount | Per Cent |
| 1914 | 162.4 | 27.5 |  |  | 22.3 | 3.8 | 33.3 | 5.6 | 196.5 | 32.2 |
| 1919 | 447.0 | 21.3 |  |  | 150.1 | 7.1 | 59.2 | 2.5 | 828.1 | 39.5 |
| 1925 | 468.4 | 20.3 |  |  | 101.6 | 4.4 | 73.6 | 3.2 | 1,006.3 | 43.6 |
| 1929 | 346.7 | 16.1 |  |  | 124.5 | 5.8 | 61.1 | 2.8 | 914.1 | 42.5 |
| 1931 | 143.9 | 12.5 | 11.9 | 1.0 | 65.5 | 5.7 | 36.8 | 3.2 | 425.3 | 37.1 |
| 1936 | 159.7 | 5.9 | 150.9 | 5.6 | 347.2 | 12.9 | 58.4 | 2.2 | 594.3 | 22.1 |
| 1938 | 312.9 | 11.6 | 316.3 | 11.8 | 536.3 | 19.9 | 16.8 | 0.6 | 425.1 | 15.8 |

|  | Great Britain | | Australia | | South Africa | | India | | Netherlands India | |
|---|---|---|---|---|---|---|---|---|---|---|
|  | Amount | Per Cent | Amount | Per Cent | Amount | Per Cent | Amount | Per Cent | Amount | Per Cent |
| 1914 | 33.1 | 5.6 | 10.9 | 1.8 | 0.5 | 0.1 | 26.0 | 4.4 | 5.5 | 0.9 |
| 1919 | 111.5 | 5.3 | 30.8 | 1.5 | 8.5 | 0.4 | 116.9 | 5.6 | 57.4 | 2.7 |
| 1925 | 59.7 | 2.6 | 47.5 | 2.1 | 9.5 | 0.4 | 173.5 | 7.5 | 85.6 | 3.7 |
| 1929 | 63.2 | 2.9 | 44.1 | 2.0 | 13.2 | 0.6 | 198.1 | 9.2 | 87.1 | 4.0 |
| 1931 | 51.8 | 4.5 | 18.4 | 1.6 | 19.3 | 1.7 | 110.4 | 9.6 | 63.4 | 5.5 |
| 1936 | 147.3 | 5.4 | 68.8 | 2.5 | 41.5 | 1.5 | 259.1 | 9.6 | 129.5 | 4.8 |
| 1938 | 135.0 | 5.0 | 69.4 | 2.6 | 35.3 | 1.3 | 188.0 | 7.0 | 104.1 | 3.9 |

|  | Straits Settlements | | Philippines | | Siam | | Egypt | | Argentina | |
|---|---|---|---|---|---|---|---|---|---|---|
|  | Amount | Per Cent | Amount | Per Cent | Amount | Per Cent | Amount | Per Cent | Amount | Per Cent |
| 1914 | 9.1 | 1.5 | 6.7 | 1.1 | 0.6 | 0.1 | 1.8 | 0.3 | 0.3 | 0.1 |
| 1919 | 29.8 | 1.4 | 18.6 | 0.9 | 3.4 | 0.2 | 15.9 | 0.8 | 11.4 | 0.5 |
| 1925 | 44.9 | 1.9 | 29.3 | 1.3 | 7.8 | 0.3 | 25.3 | 1.1 | 8.5 | 0.4 |
| 1929 | 27.9 | 1.3 | 30.6 | 1.4 | 10.6 | 0.5 | 31.4 | 1.5 | 8.6 | 0.4 |
| 1931 | 19.1 | 1.7 | 20.4 | 1.8 | 4.7 | 0.4 | 22.8 | 2.0 | 4.7 | 0.4 |
| 1936 | 58.8 | 2.3 | 51.8 | 1.2 | 43.0 | 1.5 | 40.9 | 1.5 | 22.7 | 0.8 |
| 1938 | 20.7 | 0.8 | 32.6 | 1.2 | 39.3 | 1.5 | 14.0 | 0.5 | 19.6 | 0.7 |

## TABLE 14

### JAPAN: TRADE WITH PRINCIPAL COUNTRIES IN 1936[1]

#### (In million yen)

| | Exports | Imports | Balance of Trade | Per Cent of Total Japanese Exports | Per Cent of Total Japanese Imports |
|---|---|---|---|---|---|
| Total...................... | 2,693.0 | 2,764.0 | − 71.0 | 100.0 | 100.0 |
| British Empire............... | 767.1 | 881.8 | −114.7 | 28.3 | 31.9 |
| Great Britain.............. | 147.3 | 72.9 | + 74.4 | 5.4 | 2.6 |
| Dominions................. | 144.2 | 299.8 | −155.6 | 5.3 | 10.8 |
| Australia............... | 68.8 | 181.9 | −113.1 | | |
| South Africa........... | 41.5 | 22.6 | + 18.9 | | |
| New Zealand........... | 16.7 | 22.0 | − 5.3 | | |
| Canada................ | 14.6 | 73.2 | − 58.6 | | |
| Eire.................... | 2.6 | 0.1 | + 2.5 | | |
| Colonies.................. | 463.7 | 507.7 | − 44.0 | 17.2 | 18.4 |
| India................. | 259.1 | 372.0 | −112.9 | | |
| Straits Settlements........ | 58.8 | 41.2 | + 17.6 | | |
| Hongkong.............. | 58.4 | 3.3 | + 55.1 | | |
| Kenya, Uganda and Tanganyika............ | 30.6 | 29.9 | + 0.7 | | |
| Aden.................. | 13.9 | 0.4 | + 13.5 | | |
| Ceylon................ | 13.8 | 2.6 | + 11.4 | | |
| Nigeria................ | 7.0 | 0.1 | + 6.9 | | |
| Palestine.............. | 5.4 | 0.1 | + 5.3 | | |
| Gold Coast............. | 3.6 | 0.4 | + 3.2 | | |
| British Malaya.......... | 2.4 | 39.1 | − 36.7 | | |
| Gibraltar............... | 2.2 | [2] | + 2.2 | | |
| Malta.................. | 1.5 | [2] | + 1.5 | | |
| Trinidad and Tobago..... | 1.3 | 0.1 | + 1.2 | | |
| Jamaica................ | 1.2 | [2] | + 1.2 | | |
| Mauritius.............. | 1.0 | 0.2 | + 0.8 | | |
| Cyprus................ | 0.8 | 0.2 | + 0.6 | | |
| Fiji.................... | 0.8 | 0.1 | + 0.7 | | |
| British Guiana.......... | 0.7 | [2] | + 0.7 | | |
| British Borneo........... | 0.5 | 15.7 | − 15.2 | | |
| Gilbert and Ellice Is. ..... | 0.4 | 2.3 | − 1.9 | | |
| Sierra Leone............ | 0.3 | ... | + 0.3 | | |
| United States and possessions... | 658.4 | 884.2 | −225.8 | 24.5 | 31.9 |
| United States.............. | 594.3 | 847.5 | −253.2 | 22.1 | 30.7 |
| Colonies.................. | 64.1 | 36.7 | + 27.4 | 2.4 | 1.3 |
| Philippines............. | 51.8 | 36.3 | + 15.5 | | |
| Hawaii................. | 9.3 | 0.3 | + 9.0 | | |
| Puerto Rico............. | 2.3 | 0.1 | + 2.2 | | |
| Canal Zone............. | 0.7 | [2] | + 0.7 | | |

[1] The word "colonies" is used here to denote all possessions which are not fully self-governing. Group totals are in fact slightly larger than shown, as Japanese statistics do not list separately all of the smaller colonial possessions.

[2] Less than ¥100,000.

TABLE 14 (*Continued*)

| | Exports | Imports | Balance of Trade | Per Cent of Total Japanese Exports | Imports |
|---|---|---|---|---|---|
| Netherlands and possessions.... | 151.3 | 118.1 | + 33.2 | 5.6 | 4.3 |
| Netherlands............... | 15.4 | 4.6 | + 10.8 | 0.6 | 0.2 |
| Colonies.................. | 135.9 | 113.5 | + 22.4 | 5.0 | 4.1 |
| Netherlands India........ | 129.5 | 113.5 | + 16.0 | | |
| Curaçao................ | 5.1 | 2 | + 5.1 | | |
| Dutch Guiana............ | 1.3 | ... | + 1.3 | | |
| French Empire............... | 88.8 | 45.7 | + 43.1 | 3.3 | 1.5 |
| France.................... | 43.5 | 19.9 | + 23.6 | 1.6 | 0.7 |
| Colonies.................. | 45.3 | 22.5 | + 22.8 | 1.7 | 0.8 |
| French Morocco.......... | 20.5 | 0.9 | + 19.6 | | |
| Syria.................. | 13.1 | 2 | + 13.1 | | |
| Indo-China.............. | 4.7 | 20.2 | − 15.5 | | |
| French Somali........... | 2.6 | 0.3 | + 2.3 | | |
| Senegal................. | 2.1 | 2 | + 2.1 | | |
| Algeria................. | 1.1 | 0.6 | + 0.5 | | |
| New Caledonia........... | 0.5 | 0.3 | + 0.2 | | |
| Tunis................... | 0.4 | 2 | + 0.4 | | |
| Madagascar and Reunion.. | 0.3 | 0.2 | + 0.1 | | |
| Society Is. .............. | 2 | 3.3 | − 3.3 | | |
| Belgium and possessions....... | 23.8 | 16.6 | + 7.2 | 0.9 | 0.6 |
| Belgium-Luxemburg........ | 16.2 | 16.0 | + 0.2 | | |
| Belgian Congo............ | 7.6 | 0.6 | + 7.0 | | |
| Italian Empire.............. | 5.5 | 7.8 | − 2.3 | 0.2 | 0.3 |
| Italy..................... | 4.5 | 3.8 | + 0.7 | | |
| Colonies................. | 1.0 | 4.0 | − 3.0 | | |
| Italian Somali........... | 2 | 2.9 | − 2.9 | | |
| Libya................... | 1.0 | 2 | + 1.0 | | |
| Eritrea................. | 2 | 1.1 | − 1.1 | | |
| Other colonies.............. | 29.8 | 2.2 | + 27.6 | 1.1 | 0.1 |
| Anglo-Egyptian Sudan...... | 11.9 | 1.4 | + 10.5 | | |
| Mozambique (Port.)........ | 10.9 | 0.6 | + 10.3 | | |
| Cameroons (Br. and Fr.)..... | 3.1 | ... | + 3.1 | | |
| Spanish Morocco.......... | 1.6 | 2 | + 1.6 | | |
| Canary Is. (Sp.)........... | 1.4 | ... | + 1.4 | | |
| New Guinea (Br. and Dutch). | 0.9 | 0.2 | + 0.7 | | |
| Other countries: | | | | | |
| Asia | | | | | |
| Manchuria............... | 498.1 | 239.4 | +258.7 | 18.5 | 8.6 |
| Manchukuo............. | 150.9 | 205.6 | − 54.7 | | |
| Kwantung.............. | 347.2 | 33.8 | +313.4 | | |
| China.................... | 159.7 | 154.8 | + 4.9 | 5.9 | 5.6 |
| Siam.................... | 43.0 | 8.8 | + 34.2 | | |
| U. S. S. R. (incl. European Russia)................. | 31.4 | 21.3 | + 10.1 | | |
| Iraq..................... | 19.0 | 2.9 | + 16.1 | | |
| Iran..................... | 4.7 | 1.6 | + 3.1 | | |
| Turkey................... | 4.3 | 4.5 | − 0.2 | | |

TABLE 14 (*Continued*)

| | Exports | Imports | Balance of Trade | Per Cent of Total Japanese Exports | Imports |
|---|---|---|---|---|---|
| Europe | | | | | |
| Germany................. | 35.1 | 115.5 | − 80.4 | 1.3 | 4.2 |
| Sweden.................. | 8.8 | 23.1 | − 14.3 | | |
| Norway.................. | 6.2 | 17.9 | − 11.7 | | |
| Finland................. | 3.2 | 6.6 | − 3.4 | | |
| Switzerland.............. | 0.8 | 14.0 | − 13.2 | | |
| Latin America | | | | | |
| Argentina................ | 22.7 | 30.0 | − 7.3 | | |
| Panama................. | 9.5 | [2] | + 9.5 | | |
| Brazil................... | 8.8 | 47.4 | − 38.6 | | |
| Uruguay................. | 7.9 | 9.5 | − 1.6 | | |
| Venezuela............... | 7.8 | 0.1 | + 7.7 | | |
| Chile................... | 7.4 | 10.0 | − 2.6 | | |
| Mexico.................. | 7.2 | 18.7 | − 11.5 | | |
| Peru.................... | 6.2 | 13.0 | − 6.8 | | |
| Africa | | | | | |
| Egypt................... | 40.9 | 45.7 | − 4.8 | | |
| | | | | | |
| Total of British, American, French, Dutch, Belgian and Italian empires........... | 1,694.9 | 1,954.2 | −259.3 | 63.0 | 70.7 |
| Self-governing countries (metropolitan countries and British dominions)........... | 977.3 | 1,269.2 | −291.9 | 36.3 | 46.1 |
| Colonies.................. | 717.6 | 685.0 | + 32.6 | 26.7 | 24.7 |
| Other colonies.............. | 29.8 | 2.2 | + 27.6 | 1.1 | 0.1 |
| Total colonies............... | 747.4 | 687.2 | + 60.2 | 27.8 | 24.8 |

# INDEX

87